Does My Vest Make Me Look Fat?

A Soldier's Year in Iraq

John Ready
Major, U.S. Army Reserve - Retired

Copyright 2013 John Ready

Cover photograph by Varano Photography, Rome, NY.

All other photographs courtesy of the author unless otherwise specified.

Publisher: Soldier Press

Specified lines from the song "Going Home", by Mary Fahl. © Sony/ATV Music Publishing LLC. Used with permission.

ISBN 13:978-0-615-38416-0
LCCN 2010909724

TABLE OF CONTENTS

Foreword

Does My Suicide Vest Make Me Look Fat?

In September of 2001, I was just a few weeks into my first year teaching at the U.S. Air Force Academy; as the "new guy," I was assigned to teach the 7:30 a.m. accounting class. As I prepared for my lecture that September 11, a colleague told me that an airplane had just impacted the World Trade Center. He also said, "I think we're under attack."

I rushed to my classroom and found 40 scared and confused cadets. We sat together in silence and watched a second plane hit the other tower. After what seemed to be hours, one cadet broke the quiet. "Captain Haynie," she said, "this is going to change everything, isn't it?" I responded, "For all of you...forever." In the months that followed, each and every one of those 40 cadets found themselves deployed somewhere in the world, engaged in the "War on Terror."

And while it's right to say that the events of 9/11 impacted every American in some way, the truth is that a very small minority of our citizens have shouldered the burden of the longest sustained period of combat ever experienced by the U.S. military. That burden has been formidable. Over the past 12 years, more than 3 million American men and women have committed their talents and sacrificed their innocence engaged in a decade-long battle rooted in the events of 9/11.

It goes without saying that war and its consequences represent a profoundly desperate dimension of the human experience. It's for this reason that when we talk about those who have served and their experiences at war, the discourse is often sobering. It's a narrative defined by terms like friendly fire, improvised explosive device, traumatic brain injury, post-traumatic stress, suicide, homelessness and unemployment. It's a narrative that elicits an emotional response – from both those who have served and those who have not – that is more often than not characterized as decidedly dark and hopeless. It's a narrative that, by itself, works against hope and healing.

1

John Ready wasn't in my accounting class on 9/11, but he was one of those many Americans who found his life forever changed by the events of that day. He had volunteered for military service in peacetime, before 9/11, as a member of the U.S. Army Reserve. Like so many others, it wasn't long after 9/11 that he found himself in Iraq, assigned as a Civil Affairs officer. John's time in Iraq was, to paraphrase the Grateful Dead, a "long, strange trip," that he recounts artfully and often humorously in *"Does My Suicide Vest Make Me Look Fat?"*

Many of us shudder at the notion of finding humor in war; however, John shares his experiences at war in a way that is humbling, healing, and hopeful – *because* it's funny. In other words, these stories grant you permission to laugh, and by doing so, he empowers his readers to take a step toward making sense of a series of events that are objectively beyond sensible. Put differently, John's satirical and sometimes twisted narrative is, in the end, profoundly healing.

Comedy has long played a role in healing the social and cultural fabric of the nation. After 9/11, many thought there was no place for humor in the context of the war on terror. However, we know now that humor and satire played an important role in cultivating both national unity and a sense of normalcy in the face of unthinkable tragedy. It started with David Letterman's return to the airwaves and his emotional tribute to New York City, and then tentatively but purposefully other comedic voices - like Jon Stewart and Jay Leno – began to leverage humor as a means to heal a nation and propel a people toward an ideal of service and citizenship. Robert Siegel, editor of the satirical weekly newspaper *The Onion*, said that, "Many things about America changed, but you can't kill humor, any more than you can kill a human emotion."

In *"Does My Suicide Vest Make Me Look Fat?"* John Ready demonstrates an intimate understanding of how and why you sometimes just have to laugh – especially when you find yourself in a situation that is otherwise surreal. John, maybe more than most wearing the uniform and deployed to a war zone, seems to have found himself in those situations quite often. In that vein, John's mission is to suggest through his narrative that "war is not funny, but that funny things happen during war." It's by demonstrating this truth that John is able, through his storytelling, to strike a balance between expressions of sadness, grief and loss, and the need for levity as a means to facilitate sense-making in the face of an inherently surreal situation.

Among the great many books that will be written by those who experienced the wars in Iraq and Afghanistan, I am quite sure that *"Does My Suicide Vest Make Me Look Fat?"* will play an important and unique role in regards to informing the public about the social and cultural narrative representative of this generation of American veterans. More than that, I also believe that John's approach to humanizing the experiences of war through humor is well-positioned to bridge the growing military-civilian divide that exists in this country.

Martin Luther King Jr. said, "Wars are poor chisels for carving out peaceful tomorrows." It might be, however, that humor and satire, as an approach to situating the sacrifices and heartaches of war and its consequences in the human experience, has a sharp enough edge to blunt future discord from which armed conflict originates. That's because war is not funny, but funny things happen during war.

Dr. Mike Haynie, a former U.S. Air Force officer, is executive director and founder of the Institute for Veterans and Military Families at Syracuse University.

Preface:

A Funny Thing Happened On The Way to Iraqi Democracy

The seed for this book was planted over nine years ago in Iraq. Its original title was supposed to be "You Can't Make This Shit Up." But after a marketing scrub, I chose the current one on that somewhat disturbing front cover.

The hangar next door to my headquarters at Baghdad International Airport caught fire, and we were forced to abandon our own building. To most of the troops on the base, the fire was merely a nuisance and a break from the mundane. To our tiny band of twenty Civil Affairs soldiers, it was the culmination of a string of surreal events and tough luck.

We'd driven to temporary housing on the other side of the airport. While enroute, we stared back at the inferno that had uprooted us from our home of the previous six months. We could see the flames poking through the tin roof, and roiling black smoke pouring out to join the darkness.

Staff Sergeant Richardson, one of the soldiers on our team, turned to me and spoke the phrase that had become our anthem since we'd arrived in Iraq. "You can't make this shit up." We all nodded.

"You know, there's definitely a book in this!" he laughed.

So, now you have somebody to blame.

It's pretty wild that someone could spend fifteen years-the bulk of my military career- training, preparing, and waiting for an event lasting just one year. One year that pretty much nulled out everything I'd learned in the previous fifteen. I'd attended hours of instruction on military leadership, how officers were to set the example for their troops. They were supposed to always do the right thing, and if they didn't, there would be Hell to pay.

In combat, the stakes were higher, the consequences greater, than in peacetime. My conception of how people are supposed to conduct themselves and perform their duties in wartime was turned on its head.

I was so naïve.

Don't get me wrong; I was no saint. I'm still not. But, unlike some of my peers and superiors, I've held myself accountable for my sins, both of commission and omission. That's all anyone should strive to do: if you do something wrong, own up to it, and take your licks. And school others on what not to do.

The chapters in this book are more like vignettes, slices of time that may or may not be in chronological order. They are actual events that happened, but I've changed the names of most of the actors in this farce. A search of books about the Iraq war obviously turned up many titles. Their common theme ran something like: "We came, we saw, we kicked their ass!" I've yet to find a memoir devoted solely to the humorous and surreal.

In the past nine years since my return from Iraq, I've had the privilege of meeting several Gold Star parents who've lost their sons during the wars in Iraq and Afghanistan. I certainly don't mean to make light of their sons' sacrifice. In fact, that fear has delayed me from writing this book. But funny and tragic stories are both about people in impossible situations, and they both need to be told.

War is a terrible thing; it snuffs out young lives, wounds people physically and psychologically, and strips away innocence. We would truly be better off without it. But until that war gene is forced out of the human DNA, nations must prepare for conflicts. And American citizens must serve in those conflicts; there's no getting around that. The purpose of this book, its mission statement, is to both show that war is not funny, but that funny things happen during war.

Your mission, should you choose to accept it, is to link arms with me as I step back through the Looking Glass.

February 22, 2013: the Army Reserve Center in Utica.

It looks quite different from when I started my deployment

here ten years ago. The building seems desolate now, devoid of color, blending into the gray skies overhead. Ten years ago it was a brick anthill of constant activity; understandable since it was a military installation and our country was on the verge of launching a war. The parking lot was filled to overflowing with vehicles, military and civilian. Today there's only one, and I'm sitting in the front seat in a trance.

Has it really been a decade?

So much has happened in those intervening years, both in my life and in my country's history. The two of us have embarked on an ill-fated excursion into a turbulent land, and emerged with our psyches damaged. Relationships, jobs, and friends have come and gone. America's had three presidential elections, and is just now clawing its way out of the Great Recession. I've retired from the military, and America's retired from Iraq.

My meditation is interrupted by the arrival of a squad car from the local PD. It pulls up behind me, lights flashing. The officer looks very young, in his early 20's, which means he was starting puberty as I was starting my deployment. He's probably just beginning his career, and is anxious to prove himself. That explains why he's decided to battle evil in a deserted parking lot, demanding license and registration of a mentally exhausted, middle-aged veteran.

"What are you doing here, Sir?" he asks in an authoritative voice.

Come on, now! We're at an armory, my car has an Iraqi Freedom license plate holder, and there's an IRAQ sticker in my rear window. It shouldn't be too hard to connect the dots, right?

I stare at the building in which I entered the biggest change of my life, what turned out to be the most traumatic experience of all. Ten years ago, we had no idea what sacrifices and heartaches lay ahead of us. But it's in the past.

I look up into the young officer's eyes. "I was saying good-bye."

"What do you mean by that?"

"Oh, it's a long story."

Meet Uncle Sugar

"The reason the American Army does so well in wartime, is that war is chaos, and the American Army practices it on a daily basis."
- From a post-war debriefing of a German General

I'll admit it: I was a fuck-up. Most of my 23-year career in the National Guard and Reserves was as far from stellar as you can get without being in a coma. I suppose I didn't take things seriously, or that I was sleepwalking or unsure of myself. Probably both. I like to think that my last few years in the service evened out the ledger, though.

Part of that lack of self-confidence was my deference to my counterparts on Active Duty; I was convinced they were superior to me because of their full-time status. They were like the varsity team, and in my mind we were like…Pop Warner. And I'll bet you dollars to donuts they felt superior to my fellow reservists and me.

Nasty Guard. Weekend Warriors. Summer Help. You name it, I've heard it.

And there were some who had no problem letting themselves be pigeonholed. "We know you think of us as 'weekend warriors', but think of us instead, as your brothers. We will fight side-by-side, shoulder-to-shoulder, like doomed Vikings!
For two weeks, then we'll go home."

Nothing like reinforcing your own stereotype…

The nickname "Uncle Sugar" was my unofficial call sign while I was in Iraq. The real one was "Peacemaker 5". I was called Uncle Sugar because I was the Pay Agent for my Civil Affairs team. This is a senior officer or NCO who is responsible for buying supplies off the local economy during a deployment. They also pay local contractors who rebuild schools, medical clinics, etc. This accomplished two objectives: the first was to free up the US military's supply and engineering assets, which were already feeling the strain of Iraq reconstruction.

The second goal was to pump much needed cash into the Iraqi economy. The bulk of the money that I paid out in Iraq was drawn from confiscated funds held by Saddam's regime, hundreds of millions of dollars stockpiled from selling Iraq's oil. This had been done through the United Nations' Oil for Food Program, the proceeds of which were supposed to buy food and medicine for the Iraqi people. Apparently, Saddam forgot to do that, as bags and bags of US currency were found hidden all over Baghdad. Who knows, maybe he was just waiting for the right time?

I'd always wanted to serve my country, mostly out of a sense of duty; but like many of the things in my life, the execution was very different from the intention. I attended the State University of New York College at Cortland in Upstate New York, where I'm ashamed to say I made The Other Deans' List, twice. I'd already spent one year there when I experienced a life-changing event: I fell in love.

She was a freshmen and I first saw her in line to see "To Live and Die In LA" at the Student Union cinema. She had these big, brown eyes. We made eye contact, and I fell like a Sequoia tree.

And that was the extent of our relationship: we never spoke. I never made my move; because I wasn't just smitten, I was yellow. We all know that is not a winning combination. For weeks, I tried so hard to muster the testosterone to meet her and ask her out. At one point, some mutual female friends pulled up driving The Good Idea Bus (I've been hit several times by it, with far more disastrous results than this dating fiasco). One of the girls told me to give her my Student ID, and she would show this to the Vision to see if she was interested. I gave her the ID card, and the next day she was forced to go home to Long Island for a family emergency, taking my card with her. The card that also allowed me to do everything on campus from checking out library books, eating at the dining hall, and signing for my Work Study paycheck.

My friend came back 3 days later, apologized for taking my ID card with her and promised to show the card to the girl right away. One week later, before we could execute the new plan, the object of my affection had a boyfriend. They got married and still are to this day.

It wasn't meant to be. I didn't realize that right away, as I was young and stupid. The fact I was young and stupid also explains what happened next.

I was so pissed off at myself for not taking action. There was no reason to think she would have liked me and started a relationship, but there was no reason to say she wouldn't, either. I didn't give it a chance, probably thinking there would be plenty of time, and that she would "wait".

So, I remember walking through the campus, feeling sorry for myself. Out of the corner of my eye, I spotted green uniforms. They were ROTC cadets, marching to a Military Science class. I thought to myself: "Hey, if I joined them that would be decisive and taking action." I could prove to myself that I was not a follower, and that I could grab life by the cojones.

So, I joined up! Like a moth to a flame, I flew. It was decisive, all right, but I had no idea what I was getting myself into.

Oh, Katie! How could you?

Fort Knox, Kentucky, June 1984. I'd been there about a week, and I knew I hated it. It was only the 6 week long ROTC Basic Camp. Since we hadn't signed a contract with the Army, we could leave at any time: Basic Training with blanks.

It wasn't as stressful as I made it out to be: the Drill Sergeants couldn't hit us, even though you could tell they wanted to.

I remember a lot of yelling. And compound swear words.

Our platoon has a barracks inspection. The drill sergeants do a walk-through and decide that I have let my country down by not properly making my bunk. Of course, to show their displeasure, they knock it completely off the frame and onto the floor.

"Cadet Ready! That shit's as wrong as two monkeys humpin' a football!"

None of my fellow cadets have had a chance to get to know each other. Good thing we have uniforms with nametags on them. Or, maybe not.

I'm sitting in the chow hall with some guys from my floor. We're wearing PTs, or physical training uniforms, t-shirt and shorts, with no identification. To make conversation, and because I hate long pauses in the company of strangers, I ask innocently, "How did we do on the inspection?"

Bad idea. This one guy from Deepest Arkansas, who I've nicknamed "Quest For Fire", shovels his grits into his mouth and croaks: "We failed the inspection. Sum gah named Radey dint make his bunk raht!" He slides his eyes over to me and fixes me with a malevolent stare. "Y'all know this gah Radey?"

I feel my heart start to pound. My fork raised to my lips, my mouth stuffed with mashed potatoes, I plead the fifth. "Mm mm."

I'm not lying; I don't know a guy named Radey. I do know a guy named Ready.

The next morning, the platoon is standing in formation outside the barracks, this time in uniform. As I stand there, I feel eyes boring through my soul. I turn and there is Quest For Fire, staring quizzically at my nametag. He doesn't seem to make the connection between my face and name; that nerve impulse was really, REALLY trying to get across that synapse, but no luck. I still feel like I want to dig a hole and come out in China. It's only a matter of time before he figures out I'm responsible for the platoon having failed our inspection.

Since we were at Fort Knox, Home of the Armor, it made sense for our drill instructors to familiarize us with the Army's newest toy: The M1 Abrams Main Battle Tank. We rotated positions inside the tank: Driver and Loader. I did fairly well driving the tank, which is to say I didn't drive it over a cliff or flip it off a road. I remember knocking over small trees, feeling like quite a badass.

Then it came time to load the gun.

I'm standing behind the main gun in the crew compartment. My job is to open the breach, shove a shell into it, close the breach and yell "UP!" I think I have it down, but the instructor feels otherwise. "Y'all better move to one side before you yell 'UP', Cadet", he drawls sarcastically.

Like a dumbass cadet, I ask why. The sergeant leans forward and barks at me: "When the gun fires, it recoils. And if you're standing back there when it does, you'll leave here inside a shop vac!"

I spend the next 30 minutes hugging the side of the tank. "Load another round, Cadet!"

"NO!!!!"

For quite a while in the National Guard, I was a Mortar Platoon Leader. My tenure was marred with accidents and near misses, which resulted in one of my nicknames: Lieutenant Magnet Ass.

Mortars are the long metal tubes that point at an angle and fire high explosive (HE), White Phosphorous (WP), or Illumination shells. A mortar crewman drops the round down the tube tail first. A metal pin waits for it at the bottom, hitting a primer on the shell's bottom, which in turn sets off gunpowder charges around the tail. The gunpowder explodes in the narrow confines of the tube and the resulting pressure sends the shell out of the tube. The number of charges on the tail determines how far the mortar round will travel down range. Inside the nose, a detonator waits for contact with the ground, enemy soldiers, trees, etc.

THOONK! One of the most satisfying sounds in the military.

If you hear "CLINK", that means the primer has only been dented, and the shell doesn't feel like coming out. It's called a misfire, very routine, but if not properly handled, will result in what's referred to as a Bad Day. The primer could still detonate.

The mortar shells are shipped with metal safety clips that keep the detonators from prematurely going off. Before firing, these are removed; else the shell just makes a small hole, guaranteed not to make an impression on the Bad Guys attacking you. In addition, the mortar round has to perform 200 revolutions before it has the capability to explode. This is another safety feature called "spin arming." It's saved my magnet ass numerous times.

During most of my career, my Annual Training with the National Guard was at Fort Drum, NY. Now there's a prime piece of real estate, situated in Northern New York, mostly flat as a pancake and downwind of a natural snowmaker called Lake Ontario. The area is where God tried out experiments to see which species would live or die. Oh yeah, only the strong survive up there. Fort Drum is the only place where I've seen bees colliding with snowflakes in April.

During my first AT with the mortar platoon, I'm helping to remove the safety clips from the HE rounds. I remove a clip from a shell, and just happen to experience tinnitus at the exact same time. I hear a high-pitched whirring noise.

"Holy shit! Did I just arm the son of a bitch!?"

"Did they tell me 200 revolutions or 200 seconds before it arms?" I struggle to remember my training from 3 years ago.

"Do I tell the other soldiers I just armed it? At least give them time to take cover before the shell blasts my bones to powder and my brains to water?"

"Can't they hear it too?"

My heart is pounding in my chest. I can no longer hear that whirring noise over the sound of it.

Panicking, I toss the mortar round underhanded away from me and the platoon. It lands in some weeds.

At the same time, a weird noise comes out of my lips; something like "NEE-YAHHNG!!!"

There's silence: no explosion. The entire platoon is staring at me.

Finally, this one farm boy who'd never uttered a sound before in my presence appoints himself unit spokesman.

"WHY THE FUCK DID YOU DO THAT?"

"You address him as 'Sir'" his sergeant yells at him.

"WHY THE FUCK DID YOU DO THAT, SIR?"
Good question!

After finally transferring out of the Mortar Platoon (I believe they held my farewell party after I left), the National Guard sent me to the Infantry Officer Advanced Course (IOAC) at Fort Benning, Georgia. This was schooling required for further advancement in my career. The military wanted me to succeed; up until that point, I really hadn't.

By this time in my life, I was married and was the father of an infant son, Patrick. I was also unemployed and money was tight, so I welcomed the chance to go and make some serious cash on Active Duty. For the first time in my career, I actually wanted to prove myself and push beyond my limits. The Army is great for doing just that, and they did. However, the training required me to be away from my newborn son for three months. He was six months old, and because I'd been unemployed during those months, he and I had been almost inseparable. And suddenly, I wanted to be worthy of him, and to finally make something of myself.

As I got into the car for the long drive to Fort Benning, I felt my heart being ripped from my chest. I was distraught. It was the hardest thing I'd ever had to do.

I had no idea how this would seem like a cakewalk nine years later.

One of the first things I had to endure after I reported to the Advanced Course is the dreaded Weigh-In. The Army doesn't tolerate fat soldiers showing up for military training. If you show up overweight and/or out of shape, that telegraphs to the training staff that you are not serious about attending these coveted schools. If so, they are no longer serious about your success, and you go home to be chewed out by your Commanding Officer. As I mentioned before, I suddenly did NOT want that to happen.

In the 2 months before my school, I'd gone on a strict diet and exercise regimen. I was determined to make weight or else. One week prior to class, I ate nothing and drank water. And I made weight, with a few pounds to spare. There was a legend going around my National

Guard battalion back in New York. It seems a few years before a certain lieutenant had reported for his IOAC pushing the limits on his weight. After receiving a cash advance for food and lodging from the Army, he'd taken a leisurely drive from New York to Georgia, stopping to party along the way with old college buddies. The morning of the Weigh-In, he got up, went to a certain restaurant, ordered the Coronary Special and drank coffee like they were gonna stop making it. Then, he went to get weighed, and was utterly shocked when he was sent packing with an official Letter of Reprimand. Oh, and a large bill that he had to pay back to the Army.

I made weight. Damn right, I did!

Once I'd earned the privilege to attend the school, I had to jump through hoops to stay in. One of the biggest showstoppers was failing Land Navigation. This included compass skills, map reading, and estimating distance, all through an infamous corner of Fort Benning called Yankee Road. Failing this course was grounds for dismissal from the Infantry School, and an ass chewing from the Commander back in New York. For the Active Duty officers alongside me, failing Land Navigation meant the end of their Army careers.

I'd never been very good at maneuvering through the woods; I was a klutz and had a tendency to panic. During ROTC Basic Camp at Fort Knox 10 years before, I always seemed to finish the Course dead last, except for the time one of my fellow ROTC cadets wandered completely off his intended compass heading. He ended up at the Gold Bullion Depository with a guard pointing a machine gun at him and yelling through a loudspeaker:

"Get down on your knees with your hands on your head! Do it slowly! Do it, NOW!"

So damn glad that wasn't me. When I found out I wasn't the last cadet in that day, I felt like Ulysses S. Grant.

So, here I am at the "Benning School for Boys", with 90 other captains and lieutenants preparing for the Land Navigation Course. The standard for passing is finding 8 checkpoints in the overgrown forest. We have to start in the early evening, so that at least some of the points would have to be found in darkness. No fun if you find them all in broad daylight, right?

As the instructors give the briefings for our exercise, several things seem pretty odd. First of all, the cadre tell the Foreign Officers:

"Gentlemen, if it's dark and you're lost, stay in one place and turn on your white lens flashlight! A helicopter will then find you."
"Please, please DON'T run away from it! It's trying to help you!"

I get the impression that isn't exactly true where the foreign students are from...

Now, we American students have to go through the course alone. Again, the Foreign Officers are given special concessions; they are allowed to work in pairs. Apparently in the not so distant past, they had to go it alone, but were given red star cluster flares. They were to pop these if they became hopelessly lost. In a notable case, one of them did, and sent up a flare while standing in the parking lot of a gas station in Cusseta, way off of Fort Benning Military Reservation. The local sheriff was a bit disillusioned.

Another odd thing the instructors keep telling us is to consult a very large map of Yankee Road mounted on a wooden platform. The sergeants tell us that our maps don't have the latest trails on them. But, the large wooden map does, and it would "behoove" us to draw the new trails on our paper maps. Besides, the trails have most of the checkpoints along them, and it's easier to maneuver along them, rather than go overland through that primeval forest.

You know, like John Ready does.

"Behoove?" I think to myself. "Where am I, in a time warp? No one says that word anymore!" I ignore him.

"I don't have time to stop and pencil that info on my map. Don't have daylight for that. I'm going to do this the old-fashioned way like I learned years ago. It kept me from away from the Gold Depository, right?"

So, of course, I fail Land Nav. The only thing that makes me feel better is that some of my fellow officers fail, too. We have one more chance to take it. It's just like Ground Hog Day. The sergeants tell us the same thing, we ignore them, and myself and 6 other officers fail. The instructors christen us "the Magnificent Seven."

Now, I'm really panicking. I'm told to write a formal letter to the Commanding General of the Infantry School, asking (begging) for another chance. I'm not able to remember exactly what I write, but a Major tells me it is Pulitzer Prize material:

"Oh, woe is me! Give me another chance, Sir! Mom drinks, Dad coughs up blood! Please don't send me home a bottom-feeding failure!"

Back to Yankee Road. This time, I stare at the wooden map board.

"Aw, what the hell, why not?" I draw the trails on my map.

An hour later, sweating, bleeding from scratches and mosquito bites, muscles sore from having to stop and rescue a captain who was trapped hanging upside down from vines in a ravine, I reach my first point. It's at the top of a ridge, on one of the trails I had just "discovered." By this time, I'm in a thorough panic; I've already wasted a lot of time. Saying a quick prayer for guidance, I stumble the last few meters and part the branches.

My prayer is answered: there's my first checkpoint! And just beyond it is the trail. Only it's not really a trail, more like a dirt road. At least 10 feet wide, but after the morass I just left, it seems like I-95.

"Should I look both ways?"

"Do I go on the green light?"

Now, the going gets so much easier as most of my checkpoints are on the magical trails carved out of the wilderness, and I finish Land Navigation with flying colors and time to spare.

It turns out that when Yankee Road was originally setup for Land Navigation Training, most of the points were placed along ridge-lines so that the students could find them easily. Thousands of soldiers have literally blazed trails along the ridges over the years. Until, of course, I and a few other blockheads show up. Apparently some students have been injured recently moving along the rough trails, so the Army widened them. Who'd a thunk?

Lesson: Always, always listen to the instructors, especially when they tap their feet and wink repeatedly; they are committed to your success.

It would behoove you to be the same.

COMBAT IS MOSTLY A STATE OF MIND

We're getting hammered. There is a seemingly never-ending surge of bodies pressing toward us. From my left and right, I hear cries of alarm as we fight in vain to hold our position. If we don't get re-supplied soon, we'll be doomed.

Every few seconds, I feel a rush of heat as the flames behind me consumed more fuel; we don't seem to be hurting for that.

Cursing and shouting fill my ears and I have tunnel vision, to boot. The crowd in front of me is also becoming more venomous. How long can we hold out? Minutes? Seconds? I just want it go away, to be back in my bed.
And then, I hear the cry: the plaintive voice from the rear telling me what I know is inevitable.

"John, we're out of Whopper meat!"

Oh, shit!

You got it: this little anecdote is not from Iraq: this is at one of my previous jobs: Manager Trainee at a fast food restaurant. I brought this up to illustrate two things:

The first is that working in the fast food industry is probably the closest you can get to war without getting shot at. The hours are long, you barely see your family, and you have no friends because no one's awake the same time you are. And, you have to deal with the public when they are at their worst: hungry.

The second point is that everybody has moments of extreme stress in their daily lives. These can last for days, weeks, and months. In my case, it lasted a year. That was the fast food job. I remember driving to work every day, dreading it, hating my profession, but accepting it because I was providing for my family. As I crested Onondaga Hill outside Syracuse, New York, I would begin to have stomach cramps just thinking of my shift that would be starting soon. That's because the restaurant I worked at was the Roman Coliseum of the culinary world. It was always in chaos; the crew came from homes in which either too much discipline was meted out, or not enough.

To make matters worse, everything in the store was constantly breaking down. The owners opted to simply jury-rig all of the important components instead of replacing them. Like the broiler, for example. The grease drain was constantly becoming clogged, causing fiery eruptions that the engineers didn't have in mind when they designed it. My first day at that restaurant, a worker began tugging frantically at my sleeve. I looked at the broiler and saw a mushroom cloud about the size of a Clydesdale billowing up to the ceiling.

Denise: "John! John! What does this mean?"
Me: "Well, I know it's not good. Call the Fire Department!"
Denise: "I don't know how!"

Earlier, on my first day on the job, two members of the crew-both 15 year-old unwed mothers-had beaten up another teenage girl in the parking lot. This was just another reason to have 911 on speed dial. At one time in my year at that restaurant, the crew turnover rate was 220%. I don't think it could get much higher unless you fired the person during the interview.

The bank next door was robbed at least once a month. A drunken customer pulled me over the front counter by my tie (the corporation did not supply us with clip-on's).
Me: "I can't breathe! I can't breathe!"
Customer: "I don't care! I don't care! Want my fries!"

One dark day, my crew committed the unpardonable sin of shorting the 911 Center operators three cherry pies. I got a phone call shortly after in which I apologized profusely for the mistake. For a while, I thought I would need to have a sit-down with them, just to make sure they would respond in an emergency.

I opened the store one Friday morning. There was just I and one of the crew. Two guys were at the tables, reading the paper and drinking coffee. The place was quiet, for once. Out of the corner of my eye, I watched an early 1980s Pontiac roll into the parking lot. I'd seen it before; this guy usually came in on Friday morning at the same time. But this day turned out differently, I think, for both of us.

A blue van screeched to a halt beside the sedan and disgorged three men with machine guns. They dragged the suspect out of his car, cuffed him and disappeared behind the van's sliding door. Other men with guns pushed the car into the lot corner and began to rip it apart, presumably looking for drugs. While all this was going on, the two "customers" jumped up from their coffee and papers, pulled out pistols and joined their buddies at the car.

Turns out the only people in the restaurant who weren't narcotics officers were me and the guy making the sandwiches...
The other employee was hiding under the counter, screaming like he was being attacked by wolves.

"He's got a guuuunnn!"

"They all have guunnns!" I yelled back.

At night after dinner, or the Crucible, as I called it, was over, I had to count the cash drawers and do the daily entries in the computer. While I was counting the cash from my shift, I would usually be wolfing down a line of sandwiches. This was because the management was allowed to eat whatever they wanted. (I gained 30 pounds in 2 months!) My options at the time were:

1) Assassinate the crew, or 2) eat to block out the pain. Option #2 was the better choice for minimizing the already astronomical crew turnover rate.

Then there was the time I had to train "Ed", a kid from the Syracuse West Side. Ed was a troubled youth from a real hard luck neighborhood. Rumor had it that he'd spent time in the juvenile lock-up. So, somehow he'd ended up in the Burger King Witness Protection Program.

Although it's August, I tell Ed he has to wear a long sleeve shirt, mostly to hide the White Supremacist tattoos on his arms. This really was not the place to show them off...

Ed's finally trained to work the cash register and it's his time to fly solo. The restaurant lobby is packed to the gunnels with angry, hungry customers. I'm fighting for my life, cramming French fries into bags and cartons; looks like half of them are on the floor. A woman is ordering a cheeseburger, but wants all the trimmings of one of the higher-priced sandwiches on it (Special Orders Don't Upset Us = Bullshit). She's holding up the whole line. "Give us a break," I say to myself. "We don't go to your job and break the Slurpee Machine!" Ed, to his credit, is trying his patient best not to snap the woman's neck, and at this point, I want to fight him for the privilege.

Finally, Ed reaches his limit. He pounds the cash register, and says, very loudly:

"LADY, WHY DON'T YOU PLAY HIDE AND GO FUCK YOURSELF!"

Well, we didn't cover this in the Manager Training Program.
Hmm...

I really believe that serving in a combat zone is a natural progression after working in fast food.

Don't Shoot The Guy On The Grey Horse

Before we deployed to Iraq, I led a team of Civil Affairs soldiers to the Army's National Training Center (NTC). This is one of the posts where Army units go to get their asses kicked and learn from their mistakes. Of course, no one really gets killed or wounded there. It's all make believe. Instead of real bullets and bombs, the adversaries engage each other with lasers in a system called MILES (Multiple Integrated Laser Engagement System). Each soldier has a laser affixed to his weapon that simulates real ammunition. The idea is to aim at the enemy soldier's harness, which is covered with light sensitive receptors. If you beam enough rays at these sensors, a high-pitched squeal emits from the luckless combatant's helmet. The only way to make it stop is to remove a key from the laser on your weapon and plug it into a box attached to your chest. Oh, by the way, once the key is out of the laser, you can't shoot anymore. You're dead, or seriously wounded. You take your helmet off and sit down and wait for Judgment Day, or at least until you are resurrected with the God Gun, a sort of uber-laser that makes all things new again, and lets you rejoin The Game.

Whoever invented that system should get a medal; nothing short of firing real bullets at a trainee can come close to teaching you to pay attention and keep your ass down. Remember, Rambo was just a movie...

Our job was to run interference for the 1st Cavalry Division in their dealings with civilians on the battlefield. These "players" are mostly retired or off-duty soldiers who meander the countryside, pestering unit commanders and reminding them that there is no such thing as a tidy battlefield; civilians get displaced during combat operations and must be dealt with. I was related a story which should be told to all soldiers deploying outside the United States.

These "COBs"-Civilians on the Battlefield-wear the harnesses, too. They may or may not carry weapons. They are very good at what they do; no training event would be complete without them. At the

NTC, high in the California desert, there was one COB who was a legend. He was formerly a high-ranking officer in the Army who retired and started another career as a COB. He was one of the original players at the NTC, and was so exulted in the eyes of the other COBs that he was their unofficial leader. He played the part of a wealthy aristocrat and rode everywhere on a grey horse.

One day during a war game, he rode out to the gate of a unit's position. He told the guard in no uncertain terms that he demanded to speak to his commanding officer.

Guard: "Go away!"

Man: "I don't think you heard me correctly, my good man. I demand to speak to your commanding officer. His troops are on my land, and I will be compensated!"

Guard: "Go away, now!"

Man: "This is outrageous! I will be back tomorrow!"

So he was. And he was rebuffed by the same guard. And the next day. And the next.

On the fifth day, the guard saw the aristocrat approach, became incensed and said something like: "I thought I told you not to come back!" He then "shot" the civilian and set off his sensor, taking him out of the action.

The man returned to the village and exclaimed: "They shot me!!!" The other players were indignant that their mentor had been struck down, and immediately acted to teach the Army unit-effectively now the enemy-a lesson. ALL of the role-players took up arms and began sniping at the soldiers as they performed their jobs. Children and grandmothers ambushed convoys and wreaked havoc on the base perimeter.

For three days and nights, the besieged Army unit was unable to accomplish its mission of supplying combat units. Finally, the Commander came to the village and asked for a truce, which was granted. The guard in question was actually kicked out of the Army; the consensus was that if he did this in training that may be an indicator that he would act this way in combat or a peacekeeping operation.

The point is that this soldier was probably never briefed that a COB would be coming around to test the Command's attitude toward civilians. Or he WAS briefed, but did not give a damn. Soldiers who are most likely to come in close contact with civilians should be trained and expected to treat civilians with respect. They are non-combatants and you should not shoot them without provocation.

And whatever you do, don't shoot the guy on the grey horse, because nothing good can come of that.

Don't Sell the Cows

"War is God's way of teaching Americans geography."

-Ambrose Bierce, The Devil's Dictionary

Big D, one of the NCOs I deployed with, was a six foot, two inch, 215 lb farmer from Northern New York. He owned a dairy farm in Lowville. Big D was very gregarious, easygoing, always joking. He'd once been in the Marines, and was very well educated: two bachelors' and a master's degree. Years ago, he'd been in a terrible car wreck, and had suffered a traumatic brain injury. On days that his hair was cropped really short, you could see the repair job the doctors did on his skull. It looked like a battery compartment door. He'd been medically retired from the Marine Corps, but still wanting to be in the military, Big D had joined the Army Reserve.

Big D knew that eventually, he would be sent to Iraq; it was just a matter of time.

He became more and more nervous as the US prepared to invade Iraq: he had no one who could run his dairy farm during his deployment. So, every week, he would call the commanding officer, and ask him if it was time to sell his cows. The CO would tell him each time: "No, don't sell the cows!"

Weeks and then months went by. The news headlines all hyped an impending war in Iraq. All of us in the battalion were on pins and needles. One day, somebody would tell us to get ready to go, and the next someone else would tell us to forget it, wasn't going to happen.

Then, one day in early February, it was official. This time, the colonel called Big D and gave him the news we'd all been waiting to hear:

"Sell the cows."

I'd started my military career in the New York Army National

Guard. By 9/11, I was an Infantry Captain, with fifteen years accrued for retirement. I needed at least five more in order to qualify for a retirement at age 60.

My selection for Major had just been approved, but now I had to find a slot to get promoted into. The problem was that the number of major slots was very small. I had three choices. The first was to find a slot on the other side of the state, or worse yet, another state. Second was to resign my commission as an officer, and finish out my twenty years as an enlisted man.

Third choice was to join the Army Reserve. I'd made some friends in a Civil Affairs unit out of Utica. They had trained with the Guard during some exercises in the past, and they seemed pretty happy. I interviewed with their unit. They told me, "Yeah, sure, you'll make Major. But you'll probably go to Baghdad to pick it up." That was, in fact, the last time they told me the truth.

Like a moth to a flame, I picked Door #3.

Friday, February 21, 2003

I've just received my mobilization orders calling me up for Iraq. First, I have to attend the Civil Affairs Officer Qualification Course at Fort Bragg, North Carolina. In order to serve overseas as an officer in a CA unit, I have to be qualified in that specialty. For the past two weeks, I've been taking a CDROM-based course in my new profession, to be followed by two weeks at the John F. Kennedy Special Warfare Center.

I head to the Army Reserve Center in Utica to draw my gear and equipment. I'm deploying straight to Iraq from my two-week school at Bragg, so I need to get everything squared away before I leave.

I'm in the arms room with the supply sergeant, drawing the M-16 rifle I'll carry in Iraq. Spotting five Squad Automatic Weapons (SAW), I offhandedly ask him which members of my team will be assigned these light machine guns. These weapons will provide extra firepower and security for our CA detachment.

"Oh, you guys aren't taking them with you, Sir."

"What? Why not?

"They're needed back here."

"What the hell for?"

"For training, Sir."

In a voice dripping with sarcasm, I shoot back: "You mean, like training for war? Right! Who knows, maybe one will come up?"

This is the first indication I have that somebody up in the chain of command is clueless and has failed to plan. As an Infantry Officer, it has been ingrained in me that every Army unit-no matter what their job or how small they are-always takes weapons like these along when they're headed to a combat zone.

The next night, I take my two young boys, Patrick and Michael to dinner and say my goodbyes. Obviously, they have no idea where I'm going, or what I'm going to be doing for the next year. They just know Daddy's going away.

I sit in my car and watch my oldest boy Patrick wave goodbye to me through his bedroom window. A feeling of dread washes over me. Up until now, I've been filled with anticipation about finally putting all my training and experience to work. A deployment to a combat zone is the ultimate test for a soldier. Now, I'm beginning to wonder if I've made the right decision, to purposefully volunteer.

My boy is still waving to me. I don't want to drive away. I'm suddenly scared shitless that it's the last time I'll see him.

He looks so small and innocent. There's a lump in my throat.

Forcing myself to shift into first gear, I drive off.

Damn.

I've successfully completed the Civil Affairs Officers Course. Now, I'm fully qualified, which is to say I did well on a few exams and stayed awake in class. I'm still black and blue from where the big rubber stamp hit me. Now, the rest of my team has joined me at Fort Bragg, and we're going through our pre-deployment training.

We're on a "training lane" where we will be evaluated on how we react to a chemical attack. This is a very real threat, as Saddam Hussein has been known to use chemical weapons against his opponents, hell, against his own people.

When the attack occurs, I, as the patrol leader, will order everybody to put on their protective masks and, lead them out of danger. I'm a bit concerned as I'm wearing glasses, and the corrective lenses for my mask haven't been issued to me yet.

BOOM! A white cloud spews out of a smoke grenade 50 meters down the trail. It's the signal for the attack. I hurriedly don my mask and adjust the straps. It's at this point that I realize just how bad my eyesight really is. Yelling "GAS! GAS!" at the top of my lungs, I start to lead the team out of the kill zone.

I nearly trip over an inert form on the trail; it's one of my troops, SGT McDonald. He's simulating being a casualty. It's my job to evacuate him. I think to myself "McDonald's a skinny guy and I'm in shape." I start to drag him onto my shoulders into a Fireman's Carry.

He won't budge. Dead weight. But I've already made the effort, so I have to follow through. I'd have to do that in actual combat, after all.

My God, he's heavy! Maybe I'm not the stud I think I am. Stumbling and nearly dropping him on his face, I carry the casualty over 100 meters to what has been designated a safe area, and lower him gently to the ground. Taking off my mask, I realize that it's not slender SGT McDonald I've been lugging, but Big D, all 215 lbs of him.

Ready for Takeoff

"I'd rather go down the river with seven studs than with a hundred shitheads"

- Colonel Charlie Beckwith, Founder of Delta Force

Green Ramp, Pope Air Force Base, North Carolina,

Our HUMVEES, painted desert tan, are on a C-5A Galaxy transport headed to Kuwait. They'll be waiting for us when we arrive in a few days. In the meantime, we wait impatiently to board our own plane, a humongous L-1011 jumbo jet.

The aircraft is owned by American Trans Air, or ATA. The airline has a juicy contract to transport American troops and cargo over to Kuwait and back; literally tens of thousands of personnel and their gear. For this service, they are paid generously by the Department of Defense.

In October 2004, after years of these contracts, after making so much money....... they'll file for bankruptcy.

Hmm. Wonder where all that money is going?

We drag our duffle bags and our rucksacks over to a semi truck, and heave our gear into the back. From there, they'll be loaded into the cargo compartments in the plane's belly. A major walks up to me and identifies himself as the Aircraft Chalk Commander, a fancy term for a babysitter. His job is to ensure everybody gets on the plane, based on reports from the units flying on this jet. Chalk commanders are usually majors; they're not too low in rank to order personnel around, but they're just low enough for some colonel to make them their accountability bitch. He needs Colonel Herriot, the senior officer in our battalion, to sign a document verifying that all of our unit's ammunition is stored in the cargo hold.

Colonel Herriot is a member of the Army Veterinary Corps, and a Reservist like me. His full-time job, until recently, has been veterinarian for New York State, specializing in animal-borne diseases. He leads a Public Health Team, a small unit which will assist Iraqi's with eradicating diseases and safe-guarding their food supplies. Because of his high rank, he also commands our unit of 21 personnel.

The Chalk Commander explains no ammunition is allowed in the cabin; our weapons will be in there, and it's not cool to have them and ammo together. It freaks out the flight attendants.

"What'll you have: coffee, tea, or a three round burst?"

The colonel is nowhere to be found (I'd be hiding, myself), so I'm forced to sign by all that's holy that the ammo will stay down below in the cargo hold. It's really a no-brainer; nobody in his right mind would bring live ammunition into the cabin.

I watch the civilian baggage handlers loading the gear. They're doing it in kind of an odd fashion: the rucksacks and bags have been dumped onto the tarmac, and then they are tossed onto a conveyor belt running into the plane. It should be more efficient to throw the bags directly onto the belt. I remark how strange this is to another officer; he explains that these guys get paid every time they touch a piece of luggage. CHA-CHING!

An unexpected development: black smoke has been seen coming from one of the L-1011's three engines. All of the gear has to be offloaded, and the fuel drained from the tanks while the mechanics work on the problem.

"The baggage handlers should be able to retire after tonight," I think to myself.

After waiting five hours, it's explained to us that there is definitely an issue with the starboard engine. However, the plane will be refueled and reloaded, and it will take us to Baltimore Washington Airport. From that point, another L-1011 will get us to Kuwait.

"So, let me see if I'm understanding this correctly: this plane is NOT airworthy enough to get us to Kuwait, but it's OK to ride it to Baltimore?"

"Nice!"

We finally board the wide-bodied plane. I'm sitting near the Chalk Commander. The Flight Engineer walks up to the major and sits down. They're loud enough for me to overhear, and the conversation is not pretty.

"We're not sure how much the plane weighs", says the Flight Engineer. "I need a final count of how many passengers. We'll estimate that each weighs 180 lbs, and we'll use another formula to figure out the average weight of the baggage."

He's not serious!

I glance nervously at the lieutenant colonel next to me. "Don't worry," he says. "This happens all the time. The airlines always take on extra fuel to compensate for too much weight."
He's way too calm about this.

"Sir, I don't think you get how crucial this is. When these things run out of gas, they glide like manhole covers! WE NEED TO KNOW HOW MUCH THE PLANE WEIGHS!" Pounding on the armrest with each word for emphasis.

Of course, the plane takes off just fine, and we reach cruising altitude. I'm starting to feel a little more relaxed. And then, I spot something that changes that. I'm really starting to worry.

Big D is sitting in front of me, flirting with one of the flight attendants. He's turned around in his seat, and in so doing, has knocked a piece of his gear to the floor. It's called an LBV, Load Bearing Vest. This is designed to carry essential items like water canteens and ammunition magazines. And, this one is doing just that.

A loaded M-16 mag has popped out of a pouch and is lying in the aisle almost at the stewardess' feet. Although she is facing it, she's yet to see the shiny bullets sticking out of one end. When she does, she's gonna go into orbit.

Oh, no!

After I'd signed the document pledging there would be no ammo onboard, the Trained Killer, convinced that Al Qaeda would be waiting for us in Kuwait when we opened the aircraft door, issued live ammunition to Team Testosterone. They're not going to be caught with their pants down! No, Sir!

Frantically, I try to think of a plan to distract her, and at the same time kick the magazine out of her line of sight. There's only one way. I reach up and push the Attendant Call Button. It chimes loudly 5 centimeters away from her left ear.

She whirls around in a flash, and yells "You big jerk! Why did you have to do that? I'm standing two feet away!"

Secretly pushing the magazine back into the pouch with the toe of my desert boot, I sheepishly answer back "I always wanted to see if those things worked."

Adventures In Higher Education

Psst! Hey kid! Wanna buy a degree? You can do just that with $400.

One of the Army's newest Major did it. No, not me!

Baby Huey was this Captain who was deployed with us. He was grossly overweight and lacked a lot of military bearing. Baby Huey was pretty much the psychotic relative that no one is supposed to see. He had been in the National Guard and Reserves since the Stone Age, and had never bothered to finish his Bachelor's Degree. He was now facing a deadline if he wanted to be promoted. I told him that he could do coursework online through the University of Phoenix or American Military University. He then told me that he was lacking 30 credits.

Yeah, that's going to be an obstacle…

But not insurmountable: about a week later, Baby Huey proudly showed everyone his new diploma. He had sent our translator down to Baghdad to purchase a degree for $400. Baby Huey was now a graduate of the University of Baghdad, Bachelor's Degree in Psychological.

Yes, you read that correctly. Turns out the translator's relative worked at the college. Baby Huey submitted this as proof of his education in his promotion packet, which I'm convinced has got to be against all kinds of laws and regulations. But, it worked for him. He was promoted one month later. I was only bitter because I'd only recently finished paying off my student loans.

Baby Huey was a thief and a liar; nothing of any value could be left around him. He was always looking to scam or pilfer anything he could sell or trade, even if it didn't belong to him. He was also fond of shortcuts, even if it put others at risk.

We're in Kuwait, about to convoy from Arifjan to another base, Camp Doha. Now, even though we have multiple bases in that country, and they are our staunch ally, it's still not a permissive environment. Extremists can still attack us. About three months ago, two American contractors had been ambushed near the gate to Doha. One of them had died of his wounds.

Baby Huey is in charge of the convoy. The first I knew that Huey was not taking this seriously was that he didn't conduct a Convoy Safety Briefing. This is supposed to occur before you leave the base, and includes what everyone is supposed to do in the event of an attack or accident, etc. I'm shocked; after nearly sixteen years, the concept of contingency planning has been ingrained in me. To ignore this is criminal.

"You're supposed to conduct a briefing before you leave the base!"

"Nah, you just wing it. It'll be fine!"

I get in the passenger seat of his HUMVEE. I'm in "full battle rattle" as it's called: Kevlar helmet, ballistic vest, protective mask, M-16 rifle, Garmin Radio. I steal a look at Baby Huey; at least he's got all his stuff on too. Maybe I'm wrong about him.

No, I'm not. After we exit the gate, we're on a straight, paved highway surrounded by desert. I've got my rifle pointing out the window, scanning for anything out of the ordinary.
Suddenly, I notice the vehicle beginning to swerve from side to side. Alarmed, I look across the cab. Baby Huey has all of his gear off, including his helmet. He's eating beef stew from an MRE packet with a spoon, while steering the HUMVEE with his knees.

"WHAT IN THE BLUE FUCK, ARE YOU DOING?" I scream at him.

"YOU'RE GOING TO KILL US!"

"I got hungry! I didn't get a chance to eat back at Arifjan!"

"So I have to die because you're famished?"

I'm Just Wild About Safwan

Arifjan, Kuwait, March 2003.

We've been at this base for a couple of weeks. Our job is to prepare for the big push north into Iraq. We're to move up there once the Baathist regime has been finally toppled and Iraq is secure. As it stands right now, the Third Infantry Division is still fighting to control Baghdad.

We still have no concrete idea where we'll be stationed once we cross the border. The Army unit that we're supporting, the 43rd Area Support Group, is planning on two locations in Western Iraq: Fallujah and Ar Ramadi. The 43rd ASG's mission will be to coordinate the flow of supplies and fuel to units operating in one of those two spots. We will support them by working with the civilian population on contracting for water and local resources, and rebuilding infrastructure.

We'll be working directly for them, but at the same time, we have to answer to our higher CA brigade and Civil Affairs Command (CACOM). This is unpleasant for us, as these two units have their collective head up their ass.

One of the briefings we've had to endure is the Rules for the Use of Force (ROE). These are guidelines for engaging the enemy. We're crowded into a large theater. The day before, several CA officers in the CACOM had been ambushed and wounded in Baghdad. This incident sets the tone for the briefing.

The CACOM Operations Officer stands up in front of the assembled throng, and begins giving a somewhat delusional interpretation of the ROE. For starters, he tells us, "If you see an Iraqi with a weapon, you are authorized to use deadly force. I want you to fire thirty rounds, center mass (the torso) into the enemy combatant!"

There were a few things wrong with this directive. One, Iraqi civilians have been traditionally allowed to have one automatic rifle

39

in their possession. So, this high-ranking officer has just given us the green light to shoot any civilian holding a weapon we happen to encounter, regardless of their intentions! This briefing is done long before the insurgency came into full swing in Iraq, so it's very irresponsible to give us this directive.

The second is that our weapon, the M-16A2, only fires a three-round burst. So are we supposed to stand there and keep firing until we use up the magazine? Do we ask the enemy to stay in one spot so that we can burn through an entire clip? Even if the individual is an enemy combatant, you don't waste thirty rounds on him.

Then, it's the turn of the Signal Officer, or G6, to brief us on our communications duties. In what he probably believes is a very rousing and dynamic performance, he yells, "You soldiers are information warriors! Your primary weapon is a laptop computer, and your sidearm is a printer! Your chief mission is to disseminate your reports in a timely fashion, so that the Command can make timely decisions!"

OK, then.

Next up is the Commanding General, Mad Cow. He just looks unstable. And sounds like it, too, for that matter: "If you see an Iraqi with a weapon, I want you to fire thirty rounds, center mass…"

I'm beginning to wonder what terrible thing I've committed in my life that has brought me together with these chuckleheads.

I've been invited, along with another major, to have dinner with some Kuwaiti general officers. On the way to the headquarters, the two of us discover that we have a couple of things in common: we both are parents, and we're both divorced. We're a bit concerned that our marital status will alienate the Kuwaitis: the perception is that Muslims frown on divorce.

We're in a quandary about how to broach the subject. Should we tell the officers, and hope that they won't be put off? This dilemma has not been resolved as we sit down on the floor.

I'm the first to "share" with the group. Remembering that Muslims love children, I hope to charm them with photos of my kids. My young sons are cute as buttons: maybe their pictures will take the sting out of the fact that I've committed the sin of getting divorced.

"Oh, Major! Your children are so beautiful! Do you have a photo of their mother?"

Oh, no! What the hell am I supposed to do now?

The courage to tell the truth evaporates, and I reluctantly pull the photo of my girlfriend out of my wallet.

"Oh, Major! Your wife is so beautiful! The youngest boy looks just like her!"
Great! I wonder just how much I've pissed off Allah.

Now, it's the turn of my companion.

"Oh, Major! Your children are so beautiful! Do you have a photo of their mother?"

"Oh no," he says. "Sir, I'm afraid that I'm divorced."

"Oh, that is too bad, Major." says one of the generals. "Don't worry. It happens all the time. Perhaps you will find a new wife in our country."

Our team is heading across the Iraq border to the tiny, but historically significant village of Safwan. This is the first settlement north of the Kuwait-Iraq border. It's also the demarcation point for the 1990 Iraq invasion of Kuwait. It sits at the crossroads of several major highways. At this point, the capital, Baghdad, is still not totally secure, and there are roaming bands of militants throughout southern Iraq. We have to keep our guard up.

Our mission is to address a problem with the water supply in the village: there is none.

The invasion has pushed any Iraqi forces from the area, and it's now under British control. Saddam Hussein, a Sunni Muslim, has used the Iraqi military to dominate the area, which is populated with Shia.

41

In the power vacuum created by the invasion, the Shiites have resorted to non-traditional methods to get water, to include poking holes in the pipeline running from the Arabian Gulf port of Umm Qasr, fifteen miles to the southeast. This has resulted in a drastic loss of water pressure in Safwan.

The first question that pops into my head is: if the village is under British control, why do we have to fix the problem? As we enter Safwan, we notice British army patrols racing through, not even bothering to slow down.

How rude!

We're still perplexed as we halt our HUMVEES in the center of town. A large crowd of children gathers around us, begging for candy. We dig what we have out of our MRE packages, and give them to the grateful kids. This makes us feel like we're appreciated, and that we've fostered goodwill in this town. Screw the Brits! They don't apparently know how to treat people.

We pull out of the village to inspect the water pipeline. Up ahead is a sign in Arabic. SSG Richardson, who's driving my HUMVEE, asks out loud, "Does anybody know what that sign says?" Deciding to mess with his head a bit, I reply:

"BAGHDAD WELCOMES CAREFUL DRIVERS'"

"What!" he cries out.

"Just kidding, Sergeant."

After checking the pipeline, we head back into the village. The kids surround our vehicles, begging for candy, and preventing us from moving forward. We have no candy left, and once the urchins realize this, they begin pelting the vehicles with stones.

My God, you're fickle!

SSG Richardson alarms the rest of us with a statement: "Uh oh! This reminds me of Mogadishu!" We all know what happened there. I'm unable to decide if he's serious, or if this is payback for my joke from before. In any case, we now realize why the Brits barrel through Safwan.

Operation Rosebud (Mustafa Had A Little Lamb)

We were in Kuwait for about 3 weeks before following behind the 3rd Infantry Division in their one-sided battle for Iraq. We busied ourselves with drawing equipment and the supplies we would need, and with coordinating with the Army unit to which we were attached. There was busy work for us also. We were given a humanitarian mission to repatriate a young Iraqi male whom had been injured in an accident up in Iraq. Turns out he was underneath his family truck, making some repairs. He left the vehicle in park and it rolled over him, cracking his all-important pelvis in 4 spots.

Ouch…

So, after about a month in an Army field hospital, the "Iraqi Patient" was released into our custody. We organized a convoy to take him across the border to his people, an extended family of Bedouins. Just before Iraq, we met up with our guides/translators: 4 Kuwaiti Border Guards. At that time, they also pulled double-duty as Iraqi Border Guards because the Iraqis had gone on permanent vacation. These Kuwaitis were unlike any others I had seen before, as they were barrel-chested and looked mean as hell. Several of them were graduates of the U.S. Navy's BUDS (Basic Underwater Demolition School). You know, they eventually become SEALs. After what Saddam did to their country thirteen years ago, they were no longer playing around. What I took away from this meeting was: "Invade my homeland once, shame on me. After that, it's open season on Iraqis."

Across the border we went, our HUMVEES screaming through the village of Safwan, as we had learned our lesson long before about stopping there and playing with the kids.

As we drove past an Army base out in the pool table that was the Iraqi desert, we spotted a maroon Nissan 300ZX with tinted windows and wire-spoke wheels.

WTF?

After convincing my driver, Batman that the Nissan did NOT qualify as war booty, we continued on until we came to several tents and dilapidated trucks. We parked our vehicles and helped the Iraqi Patient out. Instantly, more people than I thought could possibly fit in three medium tents came rushing forth. There were many tears of joy and a lot of man kissing.

The boy's father invited us into the main tent and gestured for us to sit down. I plopped down next to a pile of rags, and the rest of our team followed suit. The Iraqis, through our interpreters, told us to have a drink. I, not wanting to appear rude, drank out of the community water bowl. This turned out to be a gracious, but medically unsafe act on my part. I was violently ill for the next few days with Saddam's Revenge.

It was announced that it was time for a celebratory dinner.

The elders, through the Kuwaiti translator, told us that dinner would be ready in about 2 hours. By this time, it was already 1400, or 2PM. Because it was our first time in Iraq, and did not want to get caught out in the desert at night, and there was a war in progress, I respectfully declined.

I now refer to this as "Bad Idea Number 1".

As my polite declination was translated, the Iraqis began shaking their heads and clucking their tongues, sort of the Arabic equivalent of "Tsk, tsk". Being the sharp guy that I am, I knew instantly that I had failed my first Iraq field trip. There was serious danger of our no longer being "Flavor of the Month".

One of the Bedouins pulled on a leash, and the pile of rags next to me stood up and bleated loudly in my face.

I can't believe this! This kind of shit is only supposed to happen in The Bible…Now what?

The Iraqi Patient's father then told us, not requested, that if we would not stay for dinner, then we would take dinner with us. The intensity in his dark eyes let me know that this was non-negotiable.

44

"Sure," I replied weakly. Now, I knew that we would NEVER be allowed to bring livestock into a major military base. But right then did not seem a good time to say so. A plan began to germinate in my head. The first part was to shut my mouth...and smile.

The interpreter helped me stow the lamb in the back of our HUMMVEE. I didn't bother to tell my driver, Batman, because I knew he was somewhat of a hypochondriac. He would probably freak out knowing that a live sheep infested with parasites was in his vehicle.

After about 10 minutes of shaking hands and man kissing, we pulled away from the tents and headed back to Kuwait. It wasn't too long before the poor lamb began to bleat.

Batman: "Sir, what was that?"

Me: "Oh, nothing.."

Batman: " Are you sure?!"

Me: "Uh, yeah, just keep going."

Batman: " Bullshit, Sir! There's something back there!"

Me: "Come on, Batman. I know that I'm an officer, but you will have to learn to trust me. Just keep driving."

Back through the Kuwait border checkpoint we went. Looking in the side mirror, I could see 3 Kuwaiti Guards staring after our vehicle, all with the universal expression of "Huh?" on their faces.

"OK, here goes", I thought. I grabbed the handset of the radio and yelled loudly to make myself heard over the engine noise. "Attention, all vehicles! We have a lamb on board my vehicle. There's no way we can take it back to Arifjan. So, when we see the first shepherd with a sizable flock, we will jettison the lamb. I will call out a codeword. It's 'Rosebud'. When you hear it, be prepared to stop. "

After 3 or 4 miles, I spotted my boy: A Kuwaiti shepherd with about 200 charges.

"Rosebud! Rosebud! Rosebud!"

The convoy halted and 2 of the soldiers pulled the lamb from the vehicle and walked toward the flock. They let Rosebud loose. The shepherd waved at us and simply turned away.

As we drove back to Arifjan, I could not help thinking that the guy probably started out with 4 or 5 sheep, and now had 200, courtesy of Americans like us.

Into the Breach

May 2003: Firdos Square, Baghdad.

We're on another local purchase mission in Baghdad. We pass by this open space where a month ago, the citizens of Baghdad had toppled a large statue of Saddam, with help from US Marines. There's only the concrete pedestal left standing.

Looking out of my HUMVEE window at the crowd, I see a young woman wearing a white t-shirt with bold black writing on the front:

THANKS NOW GO HOME!

Wow! They already want us gone.

If even a fraction of Iraq's citizens feel that way, just over a month since the toppling of one of the most brutal and repressive regimes in modern history, we're going to have problems in this country. Sometimes, I hate being right.

"You know", I say to a fellow Civil Affairs officer. "Even though we've won the war, there's a real danger of us losing the peace."

The other officer turns to me and dismisses my comment: "You think too much!"

Wow, nobody's EVER told me that before!

Most of the Iraqi Army has gone on permanent vacation; the majority of the troops have lost heart and gone home. Only the hardcore Special Republican Guard and Saddam's cronies in the Baathist regime remain, and they're fighting a losing battle.

Paul Bremer has just been appointed head of the Office of

47

Coalition Provisional Authority (OCPA), Iraq's transition government. He's responsible for shoehorning Iraq's bickering tribes and religious factions into a democracy. Good luck with that.

One of his first decrees is to disband what's left of the Iraqi Army. His reasoning is that too many of their officers were aligned with Saddam, which makes sense if you're purging the military of bad guys. But by letting everyone go, thousands of young men are suddenly without a source of income. Young men experienced with using weapons and explosives.

Saddam's disgruntled cronies now rush to tap into this body of knowledge and expertise. They offer $5000 to anyone who will kill an American soldier, and they get a lot of takers. OCPA counteracts with an offer to pay $2000 to anybody who turns in the guys who are offering the $5000. It's that new math.

Once we arrive at the Baghdad International Airport, our small, but ambitious Civil Affairs detachment begins assessing the population living outside the perimeter. We find that their schools and medical clinics are in dire need of repair.

Our troops begin contracting with established Iraqi engineers to rebuild them. We need to be proactive and take the reconstruction effort to the Iraqi people. If we make them come to us, the civilians will begin to crowd the gates to the base. This could possibly incite riots, and threaten the security.

Over the course of the next ten months, our troops will complete 25 reconstruction projects, at the cost of just over $2 million in funds confiscated from Saddam's regime. We have no way of knowing at what personal cost and sacrifice this monumental effort will be achieved.

Abu Ghraib: University of Baghdad, College of Veterinary Medicine.

Our convoy of HUMVEEs pulls into the grounds of the college. We're to meet up with the rest of our Civil Affairs detachment, which has been coordinating the refurbishing the university. Colonel Herriot, veterinarian in civilian life, is an obvious choice to spearhead this effort.

The groundskeeper informs us that Colonel Herriot and the others are on the other side of the compound, and offers to show us the way. Without thinking, I let him get into the front passenger seat of my vehicle.

We rendezvous with the rest of our team. Abbas, our translator, rushes up to me. He looks agitated. I can tell that his usual happy demeanor has deserted him, and that somehow, I'm responsible.

"Who is this man, Major Ready?" he asks urgently.

"Oh, he's the college groundskeeper, Abbas."

"How do you know that? Did he show you identification?" He's not letting me off the hook.

"He said he was," I say, even though I know my words are about to indict me.

Abbas just stares at me like a teacher at an errant schoolboy. I can tell I've screwed up, possibly put everyone at risk by being too accommodating.

"You don't trust anyone in Iraq," he says in a stern voice. "Don't even trust me."

This is going to be a long year.

Log Base Seitz, Iraq.

The 43rd Area Support Group is preparing to redeploy back to Kuwait. Now that the 1AD has taken over responsibility for the Baghdad Area of Operations, the unit we came to BIAP with is apparently no longer required.

Their vehicles are lined up within the moonlit compound, ready for the trip back down MSR Tampa to Kuwait City.

An elderly man arrives at the main gate. He can speak no English, but carries a hand-written note. The guards tell him to leave, but there's something about the urgency in his hand gestures and pleading that prompts the soldiers to send for a translator. The Iraqi contractor takes one look at the note, and translates its contents excitedly to an officer.

Within minutes, a Quick Reaction Force (QRF) barrels down the road to the elderly man's property. They confirm several depressions in the dirt where it's obvious something has been buried. The troops lay in wait, and sure enough, they spot a team of insurgents moving in to retrieve the contents: RPG's, AK-47's, and mortars.

The Americans apprehend the men. The old Iraqi is asked why he turned them in. Through the interpreter, he relates that the American soldiers had cleaned out the irrigation system in his neighborhood, allowing him to once again grow crops. He was grateful, and didn't want anything bad to happen to the soldiers.

The irrigation project was ours. Our team had made a difference, at least to this gentleman, and to the soldiers of the 43rd ASG. They would have been sitting ducks as they left the base and travelled that road, on their way home.

Eddie and the Cruisers

While we were in Arifjan, four Kuwaiti men contracted to be our translators once we reached Baghdad. Our attitude was "we're going to need all the help we can get." So, we accepted them into our team, and outfitted them with uniforms and equipment so that they would blend in. The four Kuwaiti nationals would be paid by the Titan Corporation, which had the contract to employ interpreters for the American military.

The four men were extremely quiet for individuals who were hired out to be Arabic-English translators. They kept to themselves, mostly, and seemed to, well, blend in.

Once we arrived in Baghdad, the Kuwaitis did a great job, translating for us while our team did assessments of the infrastructure in the immediate area of Baghdad International Airport. They were very friendly to us, but I noticed they had a sense of arrogance and hostility toward the Iraqi civilians. That's not surprising due to the fact that the Iraqi invasion of Kuwait had occurred not even 13 years before. I just hoped they didn't piss off the locals at our expense.

Another behavior I noticed was their constant interest in possible locations of Kuwaiti POW's, upwards of 40,000 of their countrymen who'd been taken prisoner by Saddam's forces during their invasion of Kuwait. One of the local Iraqi's had come forward with the claim that he knew where some of these people were imprisoned, and that they were still alive. This rumor never panned out, unfortunately. It was a dead end, but our interpreters became very animated. They subjected the Iraqi to what can only be described as a ruthless interrogation, which was way out of their job description.

We were there for about three weeks, when the Kuwaiti translators abruptly announced that they had to return to Kuwait City because "their paperwork was not in order."

I thought that was kind of weird.

"We have a fax machine. You could take care of this problem without having to go all the way through 375 miles of desert."

"Oh, no, Major. This has to be done in person. The paperwork is very, very complicated!" Achmed, their spokesman told me.

I still thought that this request was strange, but I wrote it off as a cultural idiosyncrasy, something that was confined to the Arab mindset. "Maybe they don't trust technology," I thought. Perhaps we as foreigners couldn't begin to understand.

So, we dismissed them, with the understanding that they would return after their "paperwork" was in order. Baby Huey and SFC Jones would transport them back to Kuwait City on one of their supply runs back to Arifjan. The Kuwaitis would have a week to straighten things out, and Baby Huey would coordinate with them to be shuttled back to BIAP. They enthusiastically assured me that a week would be more than enough time to remedy their situation.

A week and a half went by, and Baby Huey's HUMVEE pulled into our compound, stocked with food, cans of motor oil, but no Kuwaiti translators.

"What happened? Or maybe I should ask, what DIDN'T happen?" I asked Huey.

"Well, we took those guys to Arifjan, and their families came and picked them up at the gate. I made sure they gave me their cell phone numbers before they left.

"Six days later, I called Achmed's number. He didn't answer. I called the others, and I got nothing. The Titan paymasters in Arifjan were no help, either. It's bizarre!"

So, now we were down to one translator. We'd been in Baghdad just over a month and now our vital CA operations were threatened by a lack of English speaking interpreters.

A week later, I happen to mention this bizarre incident to an Intelligence Officer in the newly arrived First Armored Division. He broke into a wide grin.

"What's so funny?" I asked.

"My friend," he drawled. "Y'all just got duped by Kuwaiti Military Intelligence!"

"What?"

"Those four guys were probably intelligence agents, sent by Kuwait to find prisoners taken by Saddam during the invasion in 1990. You were their ticket north to Baghdad!"

I feel so used!

About one month after we arrived in Iraq, we were assigned an Iraqi-American who had volunteered to participate in the liberation of Iraq; consequently, he became one of our interpreters. A Christian, he had left Iraq 37 years before to escape religious persecution, and had established himself as a printer in the Iraqi expatriate community near Detroit. His brother was still in Iraq, and cozying up to the invasion force was his ticket to be reunited with him. He was very articulate, intelligent, and bore a remarkable resemblance to former Russian President Eduard Shevardnadze.

For that reason, I call him "Eddie". Eddie was also very ambitious. He was convinced that in the very near future, there would be scores of opportunities for entrepreneurs in Iraq. Everything from fruit to oil would be the envy of the rest of the world. "In two years, there will be so much oil being pumped out of here, we'll be able to sell off Alaska!" said Eddie.

He was also convinced that he and I were destined to become business partners. "Next year, Major, you and me will come back here and open a hot dog and hamburger stand for the American troops!"

"I'm not thinking so, Eddie. First of all, I hate this country; I wish this place was burned. Second, we already have a Burger King..."

Eddie let us know that his brother and his family lived in the Christian enclave in Baghdad. Under Saddam, Iraqi Christians had fared much better than other ethnic and religious minorities, which is to say they weren't rounded up and exterminated. The Christians were even allowed to keep their churches and to worship. They were, however, forced to remove the crosses.

We took Eddie on a mission to find his family in Baghdad. It was a joyous and very emotional reunion, I have to say. A steady stream of Eddie's family, friends and old neighbors came to his brother's house, people he had not seen in thirty-seven years. The parish priest took us on a tour of church. While we were there, the priest turned to me with tears in his eyes, and pointedly asked if we could find the church a cross that could be affixed to the roof. Now that Saddam had been voted off The Island, the churches could once again display the symbol of Christianity. I told him I would look for one.

Back at BIAP, I found a section of steel rebar in the shape of a cross. I showed it to Eddie and he was overjoyed. The next time our team went into Baghdad, the rebar cross, almost elegant in its simplicity, proudly telegraphed to Baghdad and the world that Christianity was there to stay.

Fast forward to April 2005. I'm sitting in a bar, filled with angst about the way my life has changed since my return a year earlier, and contemplating what choices I should make. As I lift my fourth Guinness of the evening to my lips, the television in the corner catches my eye. It's tuned to CNN. On the screen is footage of a wrecked and burning sand-colored structure. It looks very familiar. The news ticker under the image scrolls by.

5 CHURCHES IN BAGHDAD FIREBOMBED

My jaw drops open, dark liquid dribbles down my chin onto the bar. I can tell the guy on the next stool is staring at me, but to Hell with him. All I can do is stare at the screen, recognizing the heavy oak doors in front of which I'd presented my gift to the parish priest two years ago. He and Eddie had been overwhelmed with gratitude, tears streaming down their faces. My eyes follow the line of the broken wall, up to where the tile roof had been.

And there's my cross.

The Trained Killer and Team Testosterone

"A soldier will fight long and hard for a bit of colored ribbon"
-Napoleon Bonaparte

"War is delightful to those who have had no experience of it."
-Desiderious Erasmus

Staring at my email inbox, I re-read the message to make sure I'm not hallucinating. Unfortunately, I'm not seeing things. It's obvious that I need to put this dude in check.

I've just recently transferred out of the National Guard into the Army Reserve. For the past sixteen years, I've been an Infantry officer, trained to kick in doors, concentrate firepower, and blow shit up. Now, my specialty will be Civil Affairs, a discipline that involves working with the local population to rebuild the infrastructure in an affected area. CA soldiers help a ground commander, which I was until recently, lessen the impact of military operations on civilians. I've just been told another Infantry captain, this one from Massachusetts, has transferred to my new Reserve unit at the same time.

I've only met a few of the soldiers in my new unit, and I've yet to have a formal meeting with my new commander. He's preparing to lead a team to Afghanistan, so it looks like I won't get the chance.

Imagine my surprise when I check my email, and there is a message from the other captain to our new boss, and I've been CC'ed. The new guy wants badly to go to war.

"John and I are trained Infantry officers. We know how to shoot, move, and communicate on the battlefield. We need to be on the front lines in Afghanistan!"

Whoa!

I don't know who this guy is, but I need to short-circuit this right now!

I email back to him:
"Hello, Reading your latest email brings up several points:

Who are you?

They don't sell timeshares in Afghanistan; there's a good reason for that.

There is no "front line" in Afghanistan, from what I've heard. The enemy is everywhere.

Where do you get off volunteering me to go to combat?

Last, but not least: it's obvious that your town needs a bowling alley."

The "Trained Killer" and I eventually meet at our first drill. I'm even less impressed to meet him in person, and he makes me feel very uncomfortable being around him. He wants to get shot at.

Until recently, he's been in a Special Forces unit in the Massachusetts National Guard (Green Berets). In order to stay in such an elite unit, he has to be qualified. He fails out of Special Forces Assessment and Selection twice due to injuries. This is a program that kicks the shit out of twenty year-old soldiers, and has one of the highest attrition rates in the military. The Trained Killer last attempted it at age forty-two.

Buddy, your mouth is writing checks your body can't cash...

So of course, we end up deploying to Iraq together. Before we go over, we're sitting at the bar in a steak joint in Fayetteville, North Carolina, outside Fort Bragg. The air campaign against Saddam's military has just started. We're watching it on a big screen TV. I turn to him and say, "You know, I think the ground war is gonna be over before we get to Iraq."

"Argh!!" He's shaking his head and fists violently from side to side. Apparently, I've upset him.
Dude, if you're gonna have a mid-life crisis, buy a Corvette!

Team Testosterone is a small group of older NCOs who, until recently, have been in traditional combat units. Like myself, they've joined Civil Affairs because it increases their chances for promotion, something that has eluded us in our former units.

These guys have also entered this community because it's the fast track to a deployment; Civil Affairs troops are much in demand, even in peacetime. They're effectively diplomats in uniform, aiding civilians in areas all over the world. In fact, our battalion's motto is "Liaisons To The World".

That's where the similarity ends. Apparently, the National Guard combat arms units aren't being sent overseas fast enough for Team Testosterone. They and the Trained Killer want to go to war, ostensibly to avenge 9/11. We now know they're not the only ones who've made the mistake of going to Iraq to exact revenge. There seems to be a lot of that going around. The soldiers in this band of groupies idolize the Trained Killer because he's former infantry like themselves, and because of his commanding presence. Walks on water, shits ice cream.

The Trained Killer and Team Testosterone have been ordered to establish a CA presence at a train depot in Garma, northeast of Fallujah. The Army's logisticians have determined that this hub is critical to moving military supplies throughout Western Iraq. They need our soldiers to keep a finger on the pulse of the local population, who've been traditionally aligned with the late regime.

One afternoon, this band of brothers returns from a mission to the railhead. The Trained Killer walks into the TOC and announces dramatically that they've taken fire. The rest pour into the room excitedly.

"Sir, I got one!" shouts Pantangelo.

"Got one what?" I ask.

"I shot an insurgent! We came under fire on the highway to Garma. There were two guys standing on a wall, and I got one in the forehead!

We're all gonna get our CIBs!"

A CIB, or Combat Infantryman's Badge, is the ultimate badge of courage, and proof that you're a badass. Worn on the left side of the uniform, it shows everyone that you've been in combat, and that you've fired your weapon in anger. You possess bragging rights that are beyond reproach.

Of course, like most awards, this medal is also used as a criterion for advancement in the military, so a lot of the awardees may not necessarily warrant the medal; its prestige has been diluted because everybody seems to get one.

Everybody on Team Testosterone is determined to get one. But, there's a little problem: we're not an infantry unit. The criteria for the CIB spell that out. They also state that the recipient must be under fire for an extended period of time, not twenty seconds.

The only award I want is to go home in one piece. Call me crazy.

"All right, we have to write a report about this, so I want witness statements from everybody on my desk in two hours."

Reading their accounts, I learn that everyone in the convoy had heard a loud bang while driving west on ROUTE CARDINALS, the major east-west arterial running from BIAP to Fallujah. All of them had instinctively opened fire, at what they had no idea. It just seemed the right thing to do. But, Pantangelo swears that he saw two figures on the wall, and has gotten his first confirmed kill. He's the only one on the team who says he actually saw any insurgents.

One of the soldiers on the team confides to me that he never saw any Bad Guys, either. He'd heard a tremendous bang, and started firing to the right side of the highway. What's more, he believes the bang may have come from a white Toyota pickup that they've appropriated.

That night during the 1900 brief at Log Base SEITZ, I relate both the story of the enemy contact and the backfiring Toyota. The

ASG Commander exchanges glances with several of her staff officers, and snorts: "Sounds like bullshit to me!" A quick consult with her JAG officer produces a plan to beat the bushes and determine if this whole incident is somebody's wet dream.

The lawyer draws up a fake document relating an incident that occurred the day before along ROUTE CARDINALS. A farmer has discovered one of his goats has been shot dead, and he wants reparations from the US military.

I take the letter back to the Crack House and show it to Pentangelo. "Know anything about this?" I ask him. "This happened right along the highway you were on yesterday."

Pentangelo turns white and begins stammering: "Uh, uh, well, Sir. I never really saw anybody standing on that wall. Uh, it all happened so fast, you know."

Their feeble attempt to get themselves awards they have not earned fizzles. It won't be the last time. My newfound mission is to quash those attempts, as it seems the Trained Killer covets a CIB more than life itself, and is willing to break the rules to get it.

I hear a rumor that TK is going to try an end run around me and the colonel, who's also opposed to the awarding of CIBs to a non-infantry unit. Rebuffed by his chain of command, he's submitting the paperwork elsewhere. His exact words to my source are: "Well, this is Dave's Army, and Dave's Army is going to get what me and my friends are entitled to." Hearing this, I go into orbit.

I storm into the TOC and summon him into the hallway. Getting in his face, I let him have it: "'Dave's Army' is about to be brought up on charges of conduct unbecoming an officer, and refusal to obey a direct order from a superior, if Dave's Army continues down the path that Dave's Army is currently taking! Dave's Army is hereby put on notice! Now go back to your desk! Live in fear!"

A month later, just after SFC Morrissey is wounded by an IED at the airport's main gate, TK is sitting at his desk. He's staring at the wall, but his eyes are glazed, unseeing. That's to be expected, I suppose, considering that the back of his HUMVEE has just been sprayed with shrapnel from a roadside bomb. Physically, he is unscathed, but I can tell by the look in his eyes that his bell has been rung. The only mark on him is a furrow gouged by a metal splinter on the toe of his desert boot. If the shrapnel had gone lower, he'd have a Purple Heart, another medal he covets.

He looks down at his boot and says in wonderment: "I can't believe I didn't get hit."

Shocked that somebody would want to get a medal that badly, I'm almost speechless. I finally ask him, "And that doesn't make you happy?"

Why would anybody in his right mind purposely seek out a Purple Heart? It's a marksmanship badge for the enemy.

Eight months go by. We're in a meeting in our battalion TOC, discussing preparations for redeployment. The base is still under threat of a rocket attack, so we keep one ear glued to the radio for any warning transmissions from Baghdad Tower.

Sure enough, the radio interrupts our meeting. It's a very short, garbled transmission, and most of us don't get it. The Trained Killer is sitting next to it, however, and hears something that propels him out of his chair. He takes off at a dead run through the double doors, and out into the hallway.

The rest of us sit there shocked. We can't decide if because we're in the midst of yet another rocket attack, or that the Trained Killer has deserted us, not bothering to let us know what the danger is.

Thanks for nothing, you non-compliant motherfucker!

We follow him into the hallway, which is a relatively safe area, in that it's away from any windows. The Trained Killer has donned all of his gear, and curled himself into a tight Kevlar ball at the end of the hallway. All I see are his boots, his ballistic vest, and his helmet. At first, I have to restrain myself from kicking the yellow bastard. After all the posturing and bravado I've heard him spew over the last year, he's all talk. Big hat, no cattle.

And then, staring at him, I only feel pity. He's wanted to go to war so badly, has actually engineered that certainty. But now, after he's finally seen it, in all its ugliness and cruelty, he wants no part. He realizes his mistake, just as I've realized mine. I have no right to judge him. And I watch another axiom about war being validated: that those who beat the drum the loudest, are the first to cut and run.

The Island of Misfit Toys

Nobody Wants an IED in a Box; Nobody Wants to Ride in a HUMVEE with Square Wheels!

April 2003:

Our convoy wound its way along ROUTE RED SOX into the sprawling airport complex. We passed by blown-up buildings and heaps of rubble, the result of the attack the previous month on OBJECTIVE LIONS, now known as Baghdad International Airport, BIAP for short. Before the invasion, it had been called Saddam International Airport.

The airport had been constructed between 1979 and 1982 by a French firm, to the tune of $900 million. Graciously, Saddam Hussein had it named after himself. It was the home base for Iraqi Airways until the airline had gone defunct as the result of UN sanctions imposed after Iraq's invasion of Kuwait. There were at least five abandoned airliners scattered near the main terminal.

I saw that there were two tall structures on the airport. They had been the administration and financial buildings for Iraqi Airways. Our HUMVEES pulled into the small parking of one of them, a brown, dilapidated eight-story high rise that was to be christened "the Crack House". It certainly looked like one. The other building was called "Hotel California".

Gotta love American soldiers.

Based on the surreal and bizarre things we experienced there, I'm convinced it was constructed on a Babylonian graveyard, and cursed the next day.

I glance out the window just in time to see The Bird bank past our building. It seems to stand on its left wing as it swoops past. This isn't a real bird, of course, but a hell of a lot more graceful than the pigeons that infest our living quarters. The Bird is a C-130 Hercules transport, a nimble, sturdy product from Lockheed Martin. Its crew is performing what has to be one of the most hair-raising jobs in the world: landing in a combat zone.

The four-engine turbo prop continues in its left bank, and then abruptly flips over to starboard, pumping out flares. Farting Fire, we call it, to confuse any heat-seeking missiles that could be fired from outside the base.

I can imagine what was going on inside that plane: the passengers' total panic as their world literally turns upside down. You're absently staring at the soldiers across from you, when, suddenly, you see their eyes bug out in surprise when the plane flips over. Fifty pairs of eyes dart around nervously, desperate for any visual clues. Just when you get used to this, you're knocked backward violently as The Bird snaps over in the other direction.

When one of our guys, Batman, goes home on 2 week leave, he flies out of BIAP on a C-130 at night. Eight miles south of the airport, the plane's threat warning radar picks up 2 SAM launches, and they're headed their way. The pilots immediately take evasive action, which is to say they bank violently several times to stay out of the missiles' arc. They also fart fire, ejecting flares so the heat-seeking warheads on the missiles will have something else to mess with.

Now, it just so happens that Batman is sitting next to a window. He already realizes that the aircraft is in a 90-degree bank to the right, and he can see fire out the portal. Of course, the flames are from the flares, but our boy doesn't know that. The sensory information he's getting tells him that his death is imminent and violent.

The C-130 evades the SAMs and lands safely in Kuwait about an hour later. As was customary, Batman calls us on the satellite phone and tells us he's made it to Kuwait Airport, but just barely. I can hear the fear in his voice. The unflappable Batman is scared shitless, and rightfully so.

"When I get back to Kuwait from my leave in the States, you

sons of bitches are gonna have to drive down here to pick me up, because I'll be damned if I'm gonna take that flight again!"
November 22, 2003: the 40th Anniversary of the Assassination of President John F. Kennedy.

Has it been that long?

Hell, I was born a week later! Am I that old?

Early morning in the Operations Center: I've just returned from another long DIVARTY briefing. Pulling into our compound, I watch a DHL Cargo Airbus liftoff from the runway. Normally, I watch each aircraft takeoff because it's a wonder to me that something that big and heavy can defeat gravity and climb into the clouds. Also, I watch each takeoff because, for some reason, I need assurance that it leaves without being hit by a surface-to-air missile (SAM). This morning, I neglect tradition because I have to start writing another bullshit report that no one will ever read. I swear the Army's motto should read:

"Only WE can prevent forests."

Just as I reach my desk, I hear a distant bang, followed by a long WHOOSH, and I forget all about reports.

Uh oh! That can't be good.

There are two radios in the office. One monitors the Airport Control Tower, even though we are not aviators. The personnel in the tower are, of course, higher up than most of the airport tenants. And they have state of the art radar, so they're the best equipped, visually and electronically, to detect rocket and mortar launches in the area. Any warnings about inbound missiles would be given out on the Tower radio.

The personnel working flight operations in Baghdad Tower are from the Royal Australian Air Force. They have these very cool and charming accents. These same accents are very hard to understand, if you don't listen carefully. Because the Aussies are the first line of defense against rocket and mortar attacks, we have learned to listen carefully.

Fuckin' right!

If you hear "rocket", "launch", and "airport" in the same radio transmission, you get in the prone. No questions asked.

The other radio monitors the Force Protection Net. Force Protection is the operation charged with the airport perimeter security. At any given time, HUMMVEES and Bradley Fighting Vehicles patrol the outskirts of the FOB, while Apache helicopters provide overwatch in a circular orbit.

This is the radio that comes alive with cries of alarm.

"SAM LAUNCH! THE VILLAGE SOUTHEAST OF THE AIRPORT! THEY HIT THE DHL PLANE"!

Holy shit, it's the Airbus I just watched take off!

Just then, the Baghdad Tower channel starts getting really busy. I can only hear the tower's side of the transmission, but it's obvious the controller, a woman, is talking to the crew of the stricken aircraft. I can only imagine the terror that must be filling the cockpit.

Baghdad Tower: "ROGER THAT, OSCAR OSCAR DELTA LIMA LIMA (DHL call sign). I COPY YOU ARE UNABLE TO MAINTAIN LEVEL FLIGHT. I HAVE A RADAR CONTACT, BUT NO IFF (Identity, Friend or Foe). RESET YOUR TRANSPONDER AND SQUAWK SEVENTY-SEVEN HUNDRED, AND WE'LL SEE IF WE CAN PICK YOU UP."

Baghdad Tower: "THERE YA GO, MATE! YOUR IFF IS SET TO EMERGENCY MODE. SAY AMOUNT OF FUEL AND NUMBER OF SOULS ON BOARD."

The tower controller's voice is calm, unhurried, and soothing. I can't help but think that's why they picked the Aussies to work Air Traffic Control. This lady is cooler than autumn in Adelaide.

Almost simultaneously:

Steel Main: "WE'VE HAD AN AIRCRAFT HIT BY A SAM! THERE'S AN APACHE UP THERE, AND THEY REPORT THE LEFT WING IS ON FIRE AND BADLY DAMAGED! WE'RE SENDING OUT THE QRF (QUICK REACTION FORCE) TO FIND THE LAUNCH SITE!

Baghdad Tower: "DELTA LIMA LIMA, I COPY YOU HAVE LOST ALL HYDRAULICS, AND ARE USING THROTTLES FOR CONTROL. STATE YOUR INTENTIONS: CAN YOU MAKE IT BACK TO THE FIELD, OR DO YOU INTEND TO GO TO BALAD (Balad Air Base)?"

The loss of all hydraulics is alarming news: the pilot no longer has the ability to steer the aircraft using the control surfaces such as flaps, stabilizer, etc. He's forced to increase and decrease the power on his two engines in order to guide the aircraft. And, he has to learn how to do this in about ten minutes.

Baghdad Tower: "DELTA LIMA LIMA, UNDERSTAND YOU'RE RETURNING TO BIAP. BE ADVISED YOU ARE NOW OFF OUR PRIMARY RADAR, AND WE ARE UNABLE TO PROVIDE VECTORS BACK TO THE FIELD."

The controller must now clear the radio channel in order to prepare for the stricken aircraft to return. The tone of her voice betrays the gravity of the situation.

"MAYDAY!   MAYDAY!   MAYDAY!

ALL STATIONS ON THIS FREQUENCY STOP TRANSMITTING! CLEAR BOTH RUNWAYS. HOLD SHORT ON TAXIWAYS, UNTIL FURTHER NOTICE!
THIS IS BAGHDAD TOWER, OUT!"

The situation onboard the Airbus has the Aussie's undivided attention.

Baghdad Tower: "DELTA LIMA LIMA, YOU ARE CLEARED TO LAND ON RUNWAY 33 RIGHT."

I run down the stairs and into the courtyard, just in time to see it lineup for its final approach: a tiny, metallic speck. One side is tinged with orange. The Airbus 300 is quickly getting closer and losing altitude. The loss of hydraulics probably means he has no brakes left. I don't know how he's going to stop the damn thing, even if he does make the runway.

My stomach is in knots as I realize I'm about to witness a plane crash.

C'mon, buddy! You can do it!

Colonel Herriot is now beside me in the lot, both of us straining to see the Airbus, willing it to make the field. The jet is in full view now: red and yellow paint job, the left wing trailing flames and vaporized fuel. By some superhuman power, the pilot has his craft lined up perfectly with the runway. But he's coming in too fast.

One second, the plane is touching down; the next it disappears inside a brown cloud that envelopes half the tarmac. Tall geysers of sand erupt along the runway as we stand watching helplessly. For a second, everything is silent.

Sirens wail. The airport crash trucks speed toward the south end of the runway. LTC Winston runs up and yells: "What the hell happened?"

"I'm not really sure", says Colonel Herriot. "But I think the air shipping rates for Iraq just went WAY up."

The DHL plane has gone off the runway into a shallow ditch, dragging a barbed-wire fence, and sending up clouds of dust.

As if the SAM strike and the emergency landing aren't dramatic enough, the stricken DHL plane has come to a rest in a field littered with unexploded ammunition and bombs. The firemen on the first crash truck realize this as they reach the Airbus. The pilots, convinced that the aircraft's fuel tanks are about to explode, are forced to wait on the ground underneath them. Then, they are directed to walk in the truck's tire tracks as it backs slowly out of the field, strewn with

explosives from the battle six months before.
How can those guys walk with balls that big?

Throughout most of 2003, the power situation in Baghdad was dire. The government had maintained the electrical grid; now that the government was gone, there was no one to maintain and repair it. What's more, every time repairs were made, looters or saboteurs stole the wiring. Iraqis took matters into their own hands and made their own repairs, which invariably screwed up the electrical supply somewhere else.

In order to alleviate the strain, the US military instituted "rolling blackouts"; each section of the metropolitan area was forced to endure a mandatory power outage. They were unannounced and unpredictable.

The airport was serviced by the city's power grid, and therefore we experienced rolling blackouts, too. There was no getting around them. You just had to take it. The power line that fed juice to the Crack House was separate from the lines feeding the rest of the facility. At least we knew when the blackout was over: the rest of the airport returned to life. But we had to constantly remind the soldiers running the power plant to flip the Crack House switch on; this was in a room by itself. The troops always forgot to reset it.

The power plant was a quarter-mile away, and since the field telephone and the radios were powered by electricity, we had to take turns walking there to remind them to flip the switch. One morning, around 0300 hours, the lights at BIAP flickered on, except ours of course. It was my turn to make the mud march to the powerhouse.

As I trudged over to turn on the juice, I glanced back to the Crack House. The Air Force had erected a huge, green light on its roof, to aid aircraft in navigation. With no power, it was obviously dark.

If it was so damn necessary to put it up there, why doesn't the Air Force make sure it comes back on? It's not that difficult to notice it's off!

It was just another thing that didn't make sense that year.

When I finally got to the power house, I implored the troops stationed there, "Guys, when the power comes back on, please, please, remember to turn on the Crack House!"

"Sir, we turned that function over to the Iraqis. We'll remind them."

Alarmed, I looked through the power station door at several civilians in front of the control panel. They began to throw switches.

I looked back toward home. The Crack House lights came back on. The runway marking lights went off.

"That's good!" I yell. "Don't change a thing!"

Attention, Baghdad Shoppers!

So, our job is to shop. Sounds pretty cushy, right? Not so fast. This is shopping in a city about the size of Greater Los Angeles, 78 square miles. Baghdad has miles of paved streets, a lot of them with bomb craters.

The city is laid out in shopping districts: one area is strictly for electronics, another for household appliances, and so on. In spring 2003, Baghdad resembles a huge, dusty, smelly Wal-Mart. What's more, the customers have broken into the Sporting Goods Department, and are shooting at each other with the hunting rifles. The city is both civilized and uncivilized, at the same time.

We're on a local purchase mission in Baghdad's appliance district. All of us are very excited, as we are about to become local purchase rock stars. Abbas, our interpreter, has found a vendor who can get us ice-making machines!

We pull to the curb in front of the vendor's storefront, and immediately go through the well-rehearsed, almost mechanical motions of setting out security and pre-planning our emergency egress routes. If we get hit, or if we find out that the area has become unsafe, we need to get the hell out of Dodge, fast.

I enter the store with Abbas. Even though the proprietor speaks English, it's crucial that we have an Arabic-speaking person with us to work out the details and speed things up. At least, that's the way it's supposed to work.

I remove my Kevlar helmet and sit down in the lobby, reluctantly accepting the offer of chai, the super-sweet, blistering hot tea that Iraqi's seem to live on.

It's 130 degrees. Is it too much to ask to get served something cold in this place?

I pretend to sip the piping hot beverage. I'm waiting for the drink to cool down, which I'm thinking will never happen. Abbas and the vendor begin what I believe to be negotiations, speaking rapid-fire Arabic.

Twenty minutes drags by. By now, I'm getting nervous about the length of time the troops are waiting outside, providing security and watching for things out of the ordinary. If somebody wants to do us harm, we're giving them a golden opportunity. But that's the case whenever we come down here.

Finally, Abbas and the owner abruptly end their conversation, and the gentleman leaves the office. I look expectantly to our interpreter, and ask how things are going.
Abbas says, "The ice-making machines are actually in Jordan. He went to get some brochures from his office."

I'm in shock. "What? The last twenty minutes you were talking constantly! What was that all about?" I ask.

Abbas's eyes move toward the ceiling as he tries to find and translate the appropriate Western expression. " 'How are the wife and kids' ", he reports.

Now, I'm really flabbergasted. It's not really safe to be sitting in Downtown Baghdad; every minute that we spend here gives any Bad Guys just that much more time to find and mess with us. Of course, I have no way of knowing just how unsafe it really is, and how bad it will become in just a few short weeks.

"Abbas," I say with alarm. "Listening to guys for the last twenty minutes, I thought that negotiations were done, and we were ready to take delivery. Now, instead, I find out you guys are going camping!"

Abbas looks puzzled. He asks, "What is 'camping'?"

With the impact of a thunderbolt, the realization hits me just how different we are from each other. We're physically only separated by ten feet of carpeting, but the cultural divide between us is wider

72

than the Grand Canyon.

In the Arabic culture, a considerable amount of trust has to be established between two people, whether they're just getting acquainted or conducting a transaction. You break out pictures of your family, and in turn admire those of your counterpart. It's important to get to know the other party, and to trust them.

This, of course, is at odds with Western culture, especially America. In our country, we've been conditioned to demand something happen right away. Whether it's a Big Mac, ice-making machines, or a military victory, we want it yesterday.

Taking time to establish rapport while making a purchase is perfectly acceptable to Abbas and this merchant, but for Americans venturing into Baghdad at the start of the insurgency, it's a recipe for disaster. Trying to play by the rules here will get us killed.

Hold That Tiger...for Questioning

Once U.S. soldiers arrived in Iraq, they were apprised of several "General Orders" that they were bound by military law to obey. Failure to comply would be cause for serious repercussions.

An officer and several soldiers from one of the other Civil Affairs battalions, which was based in the Green Zone, decided to test these General Orders one night. I have to hand it to them: they really outdid themselves. Let's begin:

They ventured off of their base after dark (1), with no security to protect them (2), in civilian clothes (3), and were drinking (4),. They bought food off of the local economy (5), and broke into the Baghdad Zoo (6).

Yes, folks; we call this the Superfecta of screw-ups.

They crept up next to the cage of an endangered White Tiger-this did not violate any General Orders-it was just freaking stupid. One of the young soldiers, perhaps reliving a scene from his childhood, extended a shish kabob through the bars of the cage. At that point-I know this to be fact because I read the official report-the soldier called out "Here, Kitty, Kitty!"

Apparently tigers make no distinction between lamb and human meat, because at that point, the White Tiger took the shish kabob, the soldier's thumb and most of the flesh of his arm between his jaws. Coming to his rescue, the officer pulled out a pistol (7) he had confiscated illegally from an Iraqi officer (8) and shot the tiger (9), single-handedly setting back White Tiger reproductive efforts for the next 30 years.

Sergeant Major and the Prize Patrol

"Danny, I'm having a party this weekend. How would you like to come over and mow my lawn?"

-Judge Smails, "Caddyshack"

Colonel Herriot and I slow our running pace and eventually stop. We stretch and discuss the agenda for today: where the team will be working, what meetings we need to attend, etc. We've been running in the mornings for the past week; it's the only time we have to get some exercise, as we're busy usually up until dark.

The colonel abruptly changes his mind, and says he needs to do another couple of laps. I tell him that I'll pass and that I'll meet him back at the Crack House. He takes off, bounding away like he hasn't already run eight laps around the huge airport parking lot. But then again, he runs like a gazelle, and myself, I'm a Clydesdale. The figure in the brown t-shirt and black Army PT shorts recedes in the distance.

Stretching my hamstrings, I'm surprised by a shout from behind me.

"SOMEBODY STOP THAT MAN!"

I turn and search for the source. A sergeant major with a First Armored Division patch strides up and points at Colonel Herriot. I wonder what's wrong. Is the colonel bleeding? Is he headed for a minefield?

"What's wrong, Sergeant Major?"

"He's out of uniform!"

You've got to be kidding me.

The First Armored Division has been at the airport for about two weeks. They've assumed responsibility for the Baghdad area of operations, including BIAP. Being a conventional Army unit, they're notorious for operating by the book, and crave uniformity, even in a combat zone.

The standard Physical Training (PT) Uniform is the black shorts and a grey t-shirt with a large black Army logo. Colonel Herriot's grey T-shirts are probably at the bottom of a washtub back at the Crack House. He only brought two of them, and has been wearing the brown t-shirts, usually worn under his uniform top, while running. Being deployed to a combat zone, he probably figured that no one would mind.

Apparently, he figured wrong.

The Sergeant Major is scribbling furiously on a notepad. He acts like the colonel has committed some unpardonable offense. In an authoritative voice, he demands to know the transgressor's name and unit.

So, this is what we're up against for the next year: Mickey Mouse, splitting hairs, garrison bullshit. Trying to maintain the atmosphere of an Army post back in the States. Uniformity at all costs. The mindset that treats the proper wearing of t-shirts as a matter of national security. Take us to DEFCON ONE!

I turn to Darth Vader and decide to mess with his head a bit. It's the only show of defiance against what will probably be a year of tedious regulations and spit and polish. The sergeants major are the senior enlisted personnel in the Army who enforce the standards. It's their job to ensure uniformity, but this one is shooting a mosquito with a howitzer.

"Well, Sergeant Major, I'm going to tell you where his unit is located. See that brown eight-story building over there? Go up on the second floor, turn left and go through the double doors. His desk will be to the left as you walk in. The soldier's last name is HERRIOT, his first name is "COLONEL.""

The Enforcer jumps and his head swivels toward me. Muttering under his breath, he tears the page out of the notebook and crumples it into a ball.

Check!

He knows he's been defeated; he was so close to punishing the violator. I don't like to pull rank, but it's obvious that I wouldn't have spoken to him in this way if I didn't outrank him. He can't write me up for being a wiseass.

Checkmate!

Saluting me, he turns on his heel and strides away purposefully to battle evil elsewhere. Looking down, I spot the crumpled paper on the tarmac.

Litterbug!

There's another high-ranking NCO that really has it out for our soldiers: Sergeant Major Short Stack. He's a slight, stocky individual with a Napoleon complex, who just loves catching soldiers off guard. Most of his victims seem to be Reservists like us. Every time one of our soldier's uniforms is even slightly out of compliance, he pounces.

Short Stack has always wanted to be a policeman. I don't know this for a fact, but he's beginning to act like it. He's gotten himself an SUV with a flashing blue light on the roof. He and his driver patrol the airport perimeter, searching for speeders, something the military police are already doing.

Wow, you're really breaking some new ground there, Columbo.

I'm riding in a HUMVEE coming back to the Crack House from the airport main gate, along with LTC Winston and two of our soldiers. The LTC is sitting in the back with me. Suddenly, I hear the driver, SSG Patrinelli, call out: "Ah, shit!" I look out the side mirror. An SUV is behind us, its blue light flashing. "Sonovabitch, it's Short Stack!" We come to a halt.

He's out of his vehicle and striding toward ours. He walks up to the driver's window, and barks: "Alright, hand over your military license and ID card! You exceeded the posted speed limit for BIAP!"

He doesn't have a radar gun, so how does he know Patrinelli

was speeding?

SSG Patrinelli's vehicle has been through two ambushes, and been driven on shitty, uneven Iraqi roads for the past year, so the speedometer twitches like a hummingbird. It's impossible for its driver to maintain a constant speed.

What is his problem? He has no idea what these guys have gone through the past year!

LTC Winston exits the HUMVEE, saunters around the hood, and asks, "Is there somethin' I can help y'all with, Sergeant Major?" His tone is anything but folksy and cordial. Short Stack deflates in front of me and stalks back to his toy police car. Wild Eyed Southern Boy to the rescue! Score one for the good guys.

There's a long, two story building off to the side of the Crack House. A communications battalion has occupied it since the Division has taken over BIAP. While we have taken steps to protect our soldiers from rocket and mortar attacks, their commander and sergeant major are focused on beautification. On any given day, I watch young soldiers raking the sand around the building, and trimming the hedges.

Oh, good! Your soldiers' next of kin will be grateful you gave them such a pretty spot to spend their final moments.

Months later, around Christmas, I'm in a convoy heading back from a mission near the north end of the airport. The light is fading, and as I look south I see bright lights. This is not too cool as the enemy can use them to aim their rockets. As we get closer, I am absolutely shocked by the realization that the lights are from a huge Christmas tree! The leadership of the signal battalion has erected a huge plastic tree complete with multi-colored electric bulbs. The lights can be seen for miles; they literally scream: "Hey here we are! Aim here!"

Two hundred yards to the west, I see Frosty the Snowman outside Division Main, the nerve center for the entire Baghdad Area of Operations; there's more brass in there than the New York Philharmonic. A few rockets sent that way could decimate the entire chain of command for this part of Iraq.

Colonel Herriot complains to the sergeant major from the building next door. He gets a bizarre response. "Oh, Sir. Those guys are such bad shots! They never hit anything they aim at!"

"You don't get it, Sergeant Major!" says the Colonel. We're smack dab in between Frosty and your Christmas tree; if they miss those, they're bound to hit us. You need to take that shit down!" Of course, they refuse.

Are these guys really that stupid, or are they only practicing?

It's one month before we redeploy. I'm making my daily mud march to Division Main so that I can forward my daily reports via secure email to the Puzzle Palace, the Brigade Headquarters in Baghdad. The 500-yard walk is good cardio. But, I'm also able to build up the muscle endurance in my right arm, as I have to return the salutes of probably dozens of soldiers. Yes, inside a Forward Operating Base (FOB) in a combat zone, saluting is mandatory!

These soldiers, who probably see the madness of rendering salutes in an area where the enemy could be watching, nonetheless do what they are told. As I approach, they snap to attention and call out the Division's standard greeting.

"IRON SOLDIERS, SIR!"

In keeping with my wiseass demeanor, I acknowledge them.

"RUST NEVER SLEEPS!"

Sponge Bob and the Tooth Fairies

In the fall of 2003, we were told that there was an impending rocket attack against the Airport from the North side, vicinity Beautiful Downtown Abu Ghraib. An emergency order went out advising all units to move from the north to the south side of their building or in order to minimize the exposure.

I was made the "Rocket Marshall" for the Crack House. My job was to make sure that everyone in our complex had moved. There were some U.S. Army dental technicians there along with their commander. We referred to them as Sponge Bob and the Tooth Fairies. We called him that because he was always mooching off of us, and his hair looked like the cartoon characters.

After all of our troops had moved, Sponge Bob, a colonel, comes up and says, "Can you help me? My guys won't move."

"Sir, what do you mean they won't move?"

"They don't believe me!"

At this point, I was so pissed that I just stomped over to their quarters and told them:

"All of you, listen up! I'm giving you a direct order: Pack up your all your shit and move to the south side of the courtyard. You got 30 minutes. If I come back in 30 minutes, and you're still here, you will be brought up on charges and confined to the Stockade".

I didn't know if any of this was true, and I doubted there was a Stockade on the airport, but by this time I had worked myself into an Irish rage and didn't really care...

Well, they just started falling all over themselves trying to get out of there. As I walked away, Sponge Bob came up to me and said: "That was great!"

"What was, Sir"?

"It worked!"

"Oh, you mean that 'leadership thing'"?

Make The Bad Man Go Away!

It takes 43 muscles to make a frown and 17 to smile, but it only takes 3 to reach out and bitch-slap somebody.

-MSG William Gandino U.S. Army (Retired.)

I don't mind being called tough, since I find in this racket, it's the tough guys who lead the survivors.

-General Curtis LeMay, US Air Force

So, now we're in a real bind. The Army unit to which we've been assigned, the 43rd Area Support Group, has received orders to redeploy back to Fort Carson. In their place ominously looms the First Armored Division, which has been given responsibility for the Baghdad area of operations, to include the airport. They're tankers by definition: they prefer to rollover obstacles, and to win battles through the application of overwhelming force. They do this in combat, too.

The First Armored (1AD) has just arrived in theater from their bases in Germany. They brought with them their own logistical and supply assets, which the 43rd ASG has been providing to the units in the Baghdad AO. The ASG apparently is no longer needed, so they receive orders to redeploy to Kuwait. The major problem is that we're not going back with them. Our expertise is needed by 1AD. Whereas the 43rd ASG has been great to work with, embracing CA as an integral part of the Iraq reconstruction, and fostering mutual respect, 1AD are collectively pricks.

Of course, individually, there are a lot of soldiers and leaders in the division who seem very professional and personable, but the 1AD, as a whole have the full frontal assault mentality. Their motto is "Old Ironsides", but first impressions force us to decide it to be "Do Unto Others Before They Do Unto You." At the time, it's almost ludicrous for me to believe that within a year, I'll have the utmost respect for that unit. I'll proudly wear their distinctive combat patch on my uniform, but we ain't there yet.

To be fair, the 1AD has had to deal with a certain general officer as their commander. Luckily for them, but not for the rest of the Coalition troops in Iraq, he's left the 1AD and has been kicked upstairs. I mean, promoted, specifically to Lieutenant General (3 stars) commanding Combined Joint Task Force 7 (CJTF7). He's in charge of all ground forces in Iraq during the crucial period of the reconstruction. So, basically, he's at the helm while the insurgency grows and Iraq descends into chaos. The 1AD holds his going away party, known as a Hail and Farewell, after he leaves. You're free to draw your own conclusions.

He's made an indelible mark on the First Armored Division, unfortunately, so it's going to take some time for them to decompress and shake the bad vibes. In the meantime, our tiny band will feel the full wrath of this juggernaut.

The first time I have the pleasure of dealing with the 1AD is in early June 2003. A Major assigned to BIAP perimeter security makes a request to my HQ for 200 Humanitarian Daily Rations (HDR). These meals are similar to the Meal Ready-to-Eat (MRE) , which are issued to American forces. These meals are different in that they are sensitive to all ethnic diets (no animal content). They're given out to Iraqi civilians in dire need of food; the yellow plastic packaging has "FOOD GIFT FROM THE AMERICAN PEOPLE" stenciled on it. We've been allocated several thousand of them to give to any civilians displaced by the invasion. (When these meals were first dropped by air into Afghanistan two and a half years before, the civilians ran from them because the packaging was the same color as our cluster bombs being dropped at the same time.)

The officer has neglected to state a reason for why he needs the meals. I call him on his landline.

"I've hired fifty Iraqi's to do some work on the perimeter, and I'm going to pay them with the meals."

Big mistake. The HDRs are gifts. Says so right on the package. I tell him that workers are supposed to be paid from his Commanders Emergency Response Program (CERP). Each ground unit was allocated a portion of money confiscated from Saddam's regime, to be used to rebuild Iraq.

"Yeah, I know that. But my CERP money is being used for another project, so I'm going to use the meals to pay this other group, because I need both of these projects to be done at the same time."

"Well, if you talk to the JAG, he'll tell you the same thing: it's against the law to pay these Iraqis with something that's already been given to them as a gift from the American government. Somebody's going to jail."

He's starting to become rankled. "Well, we never had to follow these bullshit regulations in Bosnia! We did this stuff all the time! You haven't a clue as to how the real world works!"

My counterpart has failed to grasp the concept that I'm merely trying to keep him out of hot water.

"Hey, look," I say. "It sounds like you're really a squared-away guy, you've a lot of experience, and you've obviously put a lot of thought into this operation. But, I'm telling you: SOMEBODY'S GOING TO JAIL!"

"Ah, you CA pukes are all the same! Prima Donnas! You always play by the book, unless it benefits you to break the rules!" Click!

Wow! I think somebody woke up on the wrong side of the tank this morning.

Jumping in my shit was bad enough, but now he's robbed me of the chance for a good retort.

I stare at the receiver, and yell out loud the first epithet that pops into my head:

"WHY DON'T YOU PLAY HIDE AND GO FUCK YOURSELF!"

Man, what a headache! Feels like my temples are being

squeezed in a vice! It's been two days since we ran out of coffee, and I'm undergoing caffeine withdrawal. We've been buying Starbucks coffee on Amazon.com. They actually will mail packages to a combat zone. DHL has the military contract to deliver and ship mail out of Iraq, but ever since the attack on the Airbus, they refuse to come to BIAP. Instead, they deliver it thirty miles north to Balad Air Base, also known as Logistics Support Area (LSA) Anaconda. From there, the Army sends it on a much slower vehicle convoy, which makes the trip once a week. I refuse to drink the instant coffee in the MREs; shit tastes like acid. So, by this time, I'm willing to pawn all the gold in my dad's mouth for just one cup of real coffee.

The TOC doors burst open. In walks Captain Crazy, a CA officer from one of our sister battalions. This officer has always seemed a bit odd; if you look in his eyes, you can tell somebody else is driving. This is as good a reason as any for what he does now. Striding over to Colonel Herriot's desk, he begins chewing his ass. "Abu Ghraib is my responsibility! You guys are on my turf! I'm the only who should be coordinating rebuilding efforts up there!"

I don't believe he just said that to a superior officer! Colonel Herriot looks hurt. He strikes a sympathetic tone. "I'm sorry you feel that way, Captain. We're working up there is because of the Veterinary College. It's clearly not our area of operations, but as a veterinarian, I'm the logical choice to assist with rebuilding it."

Maybe the colonel will let this guy get away with his outburst, but it doesn't mean that I have to. Now my head is really about to explode!

"Let's go out into the hallway, Captain. We're gonna have a little chit chat!"

The TOC doors close behind us, and I go up one side of him and down the other.

"What the hell makes you think you can even try to chew out a full colonel like that?

"Uh, uh, Sir", he stammers. "It's universally understood that in Civil Affairs, rank doesn't matter!"

"Bullshit! He's a colonel, you're just an captain; he's got change coming! Don't you ever, ever come in here and talk to him like that again! Now, go back in there and apologize to him, or I'll rip your arm off and shove it straight up your ass!"

I told you that going without coffee is bad for me.

Captain Crazy walks nervously up to Colonel Herriot's desk and assumes the position of attention. "Sir, I'm really, really sorry! I don't know what came over me."

"Oh, that's OK," says the colonel. "We're all friends here!"

Why do I even try?

Because of incidents like this, I've developed a reputation of being difficult. "Major Ready is abrasive and confrontational." And, of course, my first reaction is "You got a problem with that?!"

Abu Ghraib: University of Baghdad, College of Veterinary Medicine.

Colonel Herriot is to meet with the dean about the ongoing reconstruction of the college. He has been without sleep for at least 48 hours. Considering the fact that two of his soldiers have been wounded this week, one can hardly blame him.

The Dean leads us into his office and gestures for us to sit down. He doesn't seem very personable today. Once he opens his mouth, this is confirmed.

"You Americans aren't doing anything to help us! You make promises you do not keep, and you are wasting our time!"

Now, keep in my mind that we've already spent close to a quarter-million dollars so far rebuilding this campus. And, as I've mentioned previously, we've had two soldiers wounded in action within the last five days. This is not the smartest thing he's ever said.

Out of the corner of my eye, I see Colonel Herriot shift forward in his chair, and his color has darkened considerably. I turn toward him, and notice the vein in his left temple standing out in sharp relief. He's reaching critical mass and looks ready to launch across the desk. I decide that I need to keep him out of jail.

"Go easy, Sir", I say under my breath. "It's not worth it!"

The colonel's show of rage has its desired effect. The next time we pay a visit to the Veterinary College, there are people waiting in line to kiss our ass. As we walk into the lobby, we're greeted by a buffet of food laid out on five tables. The Dean's demeanor has taken a dramatic turn; he greets us enthusiastically and kisses us on both cheeks. He's ingratiating, apologetic, and I wouldn't be shocked if he confessed to the assassination of President Kennedy.

Colonel Herriot, in his rage, has tapped into the Iraqi psyche: they are so used to the application of force and intimidation, they have learned to expect it. Saddam ruled with an iron fist, and he kept everyone in Iraq-Sunni, Shiites, and Kurds alike-in line. For better or worse, we've taken his place. We have to make a decision whether his method of ruling is our style, and whether or not we have the will to use it.

Mr. Rumsfeld, I'm Ready for My Close-up!

June 2003, Downtown Baghdad:

We're in the shopping district that deals in medical equipment and supplies. They're needed for a medical clinic that Captain Hammond, our PA, is helping to rebuild in Airport Village, just outside BIAP. Eddie, the Iraqi-American interpreter, is with him in one of the shops. The rest of us are pulling security on the street.

A crowd is gathering around us, getting bigger by the minute. I'm starting to get a bit nervous. Out of the mass of people, a pathetic figure hobbles forward on one crutch. His ankle is swollen grotesquely. He hands me a slip of paper with Arabic writing.

This is a problem because Eddie is our only interpreter, and he's busy. I remember Baby Huey telling me that he'd been to a six-week Arab language course at the brigade last year. I summon him.

"I can't speak Arabic", says Baby Huey.

"What, I thought you said you went to this intensive course at the brigade last year!"

"That was a gentleman's course, Major", he says. "I partied every night! My Arabic's no good!"

"Well, we got about five minutes for you to become fluent!"

An Iraqi walks up and identifies himself as an engineer who'd studied in England. He offers to translate for us. He also lets me know that he's been unemployed for years, and needs a job. I tell him that I'll take his name, and that I can't promise anything.

The crippled man, as it turns out, has had the same terrible wound for years. He's been receiving treatment at the local hospital, but that's been closed since the invasion. The dilemma we face is that if we treat him, it will have to be at an advanced facility; this injury is way too serious to be cared for by our PA. If we get him to a military

91

hospital, that will open the floodgates for tens of thousands of injured civilians. The military will be swamped.

Through the engineer, I explain to the poor man that there's nothing we can do for him. He looks deflated, the translator and the crowd look agitated, and I feel like shit.

KLUNK! KLUNK!

Something just bumped my helmet.

Pivoting to my left, I see what it is: a shotgun microphone, and just beyond it, a camera with a peacock feather logo and the words:

NBC NEWS

Holy shit! I'm from a small town in upstate New York, and now I'm on the world stage...

I turn to Baby Huey, and whisper through a forced smile, "Get Hammond! Now! Tell him to drop everything!"

Looking the Iraqi engineer in the eye, I let him know of our change in plans: "Oh, we'll help him out!"

At this point, I'm ready to do the procedure myself, anything to get that awful camera out of my face. You bet your sweet ass!

Bob Hope Dining Facility, Baghdad International Airport.

The place is obviously named in honor of the late soldier-friendly entertainer who passed away earlier in our deployment. It's a huge semi-circular frame encased in white fabric, built to accommodate the thousands of hungry troops stationed at BIAP. At mealtime, the place is swamped with hundreds of soldiers.

It serves another purpose. The Bob Hope DFAC is the default setting for Public Affairs (PA) activities. Also known as Dog and Pony

Shows, Meet and Greet, Press the Flesh, Squeeze the Cheese. You get the picture.

Most of the PA activities involve soldiers meeting with congressional representatives and senators from their respective states. They're here to see how well things are going, which honestly, changes minute to minute. I've already met with New York's governor and a couple of representatives.

Thanksgiving 2003, 1800 hours. The Trained Killer and most of the soldiers have been invited to the Bob Hope DFAC for a special holiday event. Nobody has a clue what this event is supposed to be, but they've been told they will be part of history. I don't get to go.

Stars fill the sky. I happen to glance out the TOC window. For about five seconds, a huge, totally dark shape obscures the starlight. It's like a black blanket flew by, completely blocking out the stars.

Freaky.

What the hell was that?

The troops finally arrive back at the Crack House. They're totally pumped up. They'd just had Thanksgiving Dinner served to them by President Bush. His visit had been a very closely held secret. The dark shape I'd spotted was Air Force One in total blackout: no cabin or navigation lights.

The next day, we were "ordered" to have dinner with then-Senator Hillary Clinton. We head over to the DFAC, and wait for her arrival. An hour passes, and she is still not on site. Seems that she is having "difficulty" getting a flight from Kuwait. That sucks for her, but even more for us, as we're not allowed to eat until she shows up.

Another hour goes by, and our stomachs are growling. The food stewards hired by KBR to work in the DFAC are from multiple nations. They're referred to as "The Sri Lankan Boys." They take pity on us, and pass us crackers under the table.

Hillary finally makes it to BIAP, and arrives in high-heeled shoes, a Royal Blue pantsuit, and a desert tan ballistic vest. She works herself around the room, greeting all of the soldiers one by one. She walks up to me and asks, "Where are you from, Major?"

"I'm from Oneida, Ma'am," I answer.

"Well good for you!" she says.

Why is that good for me? Is there more fluoride in the water? Are the schools supposed to be better there? Do you even know where Oneida is?

We finally sit down to eat. Every so often, I catch her stealing surprised looks at us; that's understandable as by now we're eating like fire ants.

Hmm! Bone marrow! Sustenance!

After dinner, we say our goodbyes. On our way out, the Sri Lankan Boys are vying for autographs from the Senator. They are jostling to be first in line, and sure enough, a fistfight erupts. One of the stewards has taken a punch to the nose, and is bleeding all over his starched white jacket.

My last visual impression of Senator Hillary Rodham Clinton (D-NY), is that of a figure in Royal Blue in a sea of white, yelling, "Now, boys! Stop it, right now!"

The Air Force had control of the west side of the airport. Stationed there was a Combat Camera Detachment of USAF photojournalists. Their responsibility was to capture the activities of all the units on BIAP. These men and women risked their lives to show what really happened on a daily basis, and not just what the mainstream media decided was "newsworthy." They uploaded the photos to the Department of Defense website directly from the base.

Eventually, they wanted more material to shoot, and wished to go with our troops into the villages to cover our reconstruction efforts. "Hey, Sir," one Master Sergeant said to me. "If you let us go along with you on missions, we'll get you ice cream!"

Oh, no! Don't do that! Think of the children!

"You've got yourself a deal, Master Sergeant!"

For the next three months, my portrait and those of our troops graced the official Pentagon website.

"Here's Major Ready at a ribbon-cutting ceremony! Smile. Click!"

"Here's Major Ready at a meeting with a local sheik! Smile. Click!"

"Here's Major Ready giving a grenade to a toddler! Smile. Click!

The Time For Bright Ideas Is Over

General Mad Cow had this brother who somehow got promoted to Colonel. His glasses were so thick you could drink out of them. In October of 2003, some Reserve units began getting their soft-skinned (unarmored, just an aluminum body with canvas doors) HUMVEES outfitted with armor plate. This "bolt-on armor", installed by Iraqi contractors, was based on an American design. One day, Mad Cow's brother decides to test the armor plate, in the middle of the Green Zone, with soldiers all around him. The armor plate stands up to 9mm ammo, but the bullets ricochet off and come perilously close to hitting several Americans. What an idiot!

I find it very hard to believe that someone could be that stupid, and still be alive. I mean, what if he forgot to feed himself?

Someone at the palace saw online the famous cartoon by the late Bill Mauldin, of the sergeant shooting his broken=down Jeep with his pistol in one hand, the other covering his eyes. He or she decided that it was too good to pass up. The cartoon was downloaded, printed and taped to the colonel's office wall.

He was the only one who found no humor in it. He kept taking it down, but it still seemed to magically grace his wall when he came back.

"Quickdraw", is put in charge of our redeployment back to Kuwait. He wants us to drive south across 350 miles of desert in the HUMVEES, which are pretty beat up. Several officers politely suggest to him that we should put our vehicles on trailers and transport the troops by air.

His reply: "The time for bright ideas is over".

Yes, Sir, it is. Ended just before the HUMVEE assassination…

Friendly Fire is Anything but Friendly

I'm at the wheel of the HUMVEE, heading out BIAP's Main Gate. In the front passenger seat sits LTC Winston. We're about to perform our daily morning ritual of meeting our contractors and interpreters outside the airport.

Due to the growing insurgency, they are not allowed unaccompanied access to the base, or anywhere in its interior. During the first few months of our tour, the interpreters had been allowed to enter the gate, and drive right to the Crack House. Then in the fall of 2003, Titan Corporation, who has the contract to hire thousands of translators for the US military, somehow "misplaced" 500 blank ID cards. Because of that, no Iraqi's can get inside a FOB without an escort. We have to meet them outside the gate and shepherd them to a holding area where they are frisked and their vehicles searched. At that point, they are under our control, and follow us back through the checkpoint to the Crack House.

I'm in a bit of a daze: as usual, I got absolutely no sleep last night. I haven't had anywhere near the amount of coffee required to make it through another Ground Hog Day. I maneuver the vehicle through the slalom of concrete barricades planted there to slow down any suicide car bombs.

My stupor is shattered by several loud pops. I happen to glance to my left and notice the concrete obstacle thirty feet away dissolving into a fine, grey cloud.

Oh, shit!

Both LTC Winston and I dive out of the HUMVEE like it was on fire, which I'm convinced it will be very soon. I don't even bother to put the vehicle in park. There's no time for even that. My sole purpose in life at that point is to get away from the fuel-laden HUMVEE and find cover. After witnessing the destruction of the concrete barrier, I realize that finding cover may be impossible.

They'll never find my seat cushion...

As I crawl toward a sandbagged bunker, the realization sinks in that the firing has stopped, but I don't feel any safer. I notice that the HUMVEE is still rolling slowly forward, so I run to it and put the vehicle in park before it collides with a roll of barbed wire. LTC Winston walks up to me and we exchange incredulous looks. It's not just the near miss of the bullets that has rattled both of us. It's where it almost happened.

"What the hell is going on here?" we both wonder aloud. It's daylight and we are right smack dab in the middle of one of the most heavily guarded and controlled checkpoints in the whole damn Middle East! But, somehow, the insurgents have snuck a 12.7mm heavy machine into the midst of it and opened fire? Some security!

The 12.7 is similar to the US military's .50 caliber machine gun. It is a devastating weapon. A person could be in the middle of Manhattan, and they'd be hard-pressed to find a structure thick enough to hide behind. It goes through everything.

It's also not something that you can just pick up and hide under a long coat. The thing is heavy and the barrel is long. In order to fire the weapon, it has to be either mounted on top of a vehicle, or anchored into the ground on a heavy tripod.

So, how did it get in here?

We hop back into our vehicle and rendezvous with our contractors. On our way back through the Main Gate, I ask a First Lieutenant posted there if the insurgents with the 12.7 had been apprehended.

I nearly collapse in shock when he tells me that there were no Bad Guys. An MP manning a .50 cal on top of a HUMVEE had neglected to clear his weapon before reentering BIAP. There had been rounds still in the feed tray. He'd had his finger on the trigger going over a speed bump inside the base, and fired the weapon.

This is only the first time this will happen to me.

Coming back from a local purchase mission in downtown Baghdad, I'm riding in a HUMVEE with Big D, SFC Wilkes, and our translator, Abbas. An MP platoon is providing security for us. One of their armored vehicles is behind us as we head back to the airport on ROUTE IRISH. SFC Wilkes starts up a steep incline.

Suddenly, an audible crack sounds right by my left ear. We're under fire! The bullet sounds very close, to the left of our HUMVEE. Strangely, the MPs are not laying down suppressive fire as we exit the kill zone. They're doing nothing. I hear just the one shot.

There is, however, a flurry of activity inside the vehicle. I'm shouting at Wilkes to speed up. She tries to floor it, but the grade is too steep, and the HUMVEE won't move any faster. She also takes this moment to argue with me, and scolds me in a motherly tone that she's trying her best.

In his thick accent, Abbas is screaming at me: "Where is the shoo-ter! Where is the shoo-ter!"

Damned if I know! I don't feel like sticking around to find out!

During all this, Big D, all 6 ft, 2 in. of him, is reverse crab walking over the entire interior, searching for the source of the one shot. At one point, he's in my lap, all 215 pounds of him. I remember thinking I'd rather bail out of the HUMVEE and take my chances with the sniper.

There's no more firing, not from the sniper, or the MPs assigned to protect us. We arrive back at the airport. I jump out of the HUMVEE to go find out from the MP platoon leader what just happened; or rather, what didn't happen.

The Lieutenant tells me in a subdued voice that there was no sniper, no ambush, no enemy, nothing. The soldier in the turret of the vehicle directly behind ours had had his finger on the trigger of his M-16. The HUMVEE hit a pothole, and he'd inadvertently contracted his finger on the trigger, firing off a shot that nearly missed my HUM-VEE.

The good news, he tells me, is that the guy didn't squeeze the trigger of his other weapon, a MK 19. Being the Glass-is-Half-Full kind of guy that I am, I agree with him.

A MK 19 is a belt-fed, automatic weapon that spits out 40mm grenades-that look like swollen bullets-at about 800 feet per second. It's normally used to fire high explosive (HE) rounds, and today, this guy was loaded for bear. It's effective range is 1500 meters, or just under a mile. The rounds are spin-armed. This means they have to travel 36 meters before they are capable of exploding, a safety feature that minimizes injuries if the rounds fall short. Our HUMVEE, however, was at least 50-75 meters in front of the gun at any given time.

Do the math.

Shockingly, this is the second time this particular soldier has screwed up like this. His commander now makes plans to send him to Kuwait for psychological testing.

I suppose that couldn't hurt.

Twice, I'm nearly the victim of "Friendly Fire". This is the term the military assigns to incidents in which soldiers on the same side accidently fire on each other. There are other terms used to describe it: Fratricide, Blue-On-Blue (the color blue is usually associated with any force not associated with the enemy). I have my own terms for this phenomenon, like "Why Don't You Watch Where You're F*%&$ Aiming?" or "Get Your Head Out of Your Ass!" Incidents like this are usually the result of what's called the "fog of war", or confusion in the heat of battle.

In my experience, it also applies to the fog in someone's brain.

The Attack of the Good Idea Bus

With the increase of rockets and mortars being lobbed by insurgents into the airport, the Army commanders responsible for the security of BIAP wanted us to evict Iraqis from their homes on the western perimeter, with the intent of creating a "buffer zone". Their plan was to use a policy that was written to rid government buildings of squatters whom took up residence after the fall of the Baathists.

The only problem was that these civilians to the West of BIAP had proof they were the rightful owners of the property. The Army disregarded this little tidbit of information. This is what I call the "One-Size-Fits-All Approach."

So, the Active Duty command tells us that we need to conduct a survey of the residents' proof of ownership so that the perimeter can be expanded. The only problem was, it wasn't our job. Property issues are to be handled by lawyers, specifically the Army JAG (Judge Advocate General). Colonel Herriot let them know this, but he was shot down.

Chastised, we sent a team out to do the survey, a decision that would soon prove disastrous for our soldiers. The residents on the land near the airport's west wall didn't appreciate being asked for documentation and proof of ownership. There were definitely language and cultural barriers between us, but most people can tell they're about to be screwed out of their land. The Iraqis decided that our soldiers were up to no good, and eventually, it would come time to shoot the messenger.

After the survey was completed and forwarded to higher, we thought that we were done with this nonsense. A few days later, we were ordered to send our team back out to tell these farmers that their land was to be confiscated, so that the airport perimeter could be expanded. OK, this was really not our job.

I met with some of the officers who had dreamed this up, and we had a heated discussion. This included my first successful attempt at brinksmanship.

"OK, we'll do it! Sure, why not? But you're coming out there with us! If it's gonna be Amateur Night, and we're making up the rules as we go along, you're bringing two lawyers with buckets of cash to pay these Iraqis off!"

They didn't like that idea. The job was abandoned. So, there you have it: a military operation cancelled due to a lack of interest.

We won, against our own side. Imagine what we could accomplish if we were such assholes toward the enemy!

It's about 2200, or 10PM. In the distance, I hear muffled explosions. The insurgents are lobbing mortars from west of the airport, again. This is getting to be almost routine. The rounds never make it to our side of the airport; the range is too far. Imagine listening to explosions and thinking of them as merely noisy, robbing you of restful sleep. It's weird, but this is the reality at Baghdad International Airport in 2003, where the location you happen to be assigned dictates whether you're under fire, or merely sleep-deprived.

The 1AD unit we directly support, DIVARTY (Division Artillery), has their big toys: 155mm self-propelled howitzers. They are large artillery pieces mounted on tracks, like tanks. They're silent: In order to fire back at the enemy mortar men, DIVARTY must obtain clearance, or permission, from another 1AD brigade which has responsibility for the Abu Ghraib sector. That brigade up there obviously doesn't want high explosive shells impacting in their area of responsibility, so they refuse whenever they're asked for clearance to fire. Smart men.

The enemy continually harass the airport perimeter with mortars. Once they shoot, they leave immediately to hide among the civilians in the city of Abu Ghraib, knowing full well that nobody's going to fire at them. Smart men.

I hear a louder explosion, much closer; I can almost sense the shockwave. Tensing up, I begin to think that it's a mortar landing near our building. But then, radio traffic confirms that DIVARTY has fired back at the enemy mortars before they've skedaddled up to the city.

"Righteous!" I think to myself. Time for bed.

The landline in the TOC is ringing over and over. Grumbling, I run from my hooch down the hall and grab the handset on the twentieth ring. It's the DIVARTY S5 (Civil Affairs Officer), a short captain with a Napoleon complex I've nicknamed Johnny Cougar.

"Uh, Sir. We were getting mortared out west again, and, uh, we fired back. And, we hit somebody's house, and we were wondering, can you guys go out there tonight, and see how he feels?"

"Well, I think we can put this to bed right now. He's pissed! It's not like the poor guy has homeowners' insurance with a three-lamb deductable! And, how the hell did you guys hit a house, when we've both gone through there and plotted house locations with a GPS, so that you wouldn't hit one? And, by the way, Captain: that was a stupid fucking question! Good night!"

Little do I realize that Johnny Cougar is calling on behalf of the DIVARTY Commander, a Colonel. The next call I get is from Cougar's boss. We have a short, excited, one -way conversation, and my lips never move.
Ow!

The next morning, we send out two of our sergeants to speak to the owner of the house, which is a house no more, but a scorched ash heap. Luckily, no one is hurt, and the Iraqi accepts some cash that will allow him to rebuild, or better yet, move far away.

I get another call from DIVARTY. They're angry because we only sent out two soldiers to speak with the owner! They don't think we're taking it seriously. What do they want us to do, send out all twenty of us?

Mail Call

We were in Iraq for a few months before we began to get mail. Because we were deployed outside of the United States, we were given an APO address. This is an Army Post Office that is set up in the Theater of Operations. It had its own zip code.

Needless to say, getting mail was a big deal. It was a way to connect back to The World. You could reach out and touch Home Base. I could receive letters and boxes, and know that my family had touched them, and it reminded me that I was somebody's Dad, son, friend and lover, not just a number wearing Desert Camouflage. Not just another scared shitless soldier trying to make it alive through another day.

Mail also created our earliest forms of entertainment and diversion. Not only were we delighted to see mail addressed to ourselves, but it also was fun to watch everybody else open their packages.

One day, a large carton arrived for me from my female co-workers. The other troops crowded around me and prepared themselves to make wise-ass comments about the items shipped from my workplace.

I need to pause here and mention that there were several items that were banned while we were in Iraq. Soldiers could not possess, among other things, alcohol and pornography. Now, the alcohol you can understand: we were always on edge and always around weapons, ammunition, and dangerous equipment. As much as I would have liked having something to calm myself down, the risks outweighed the rewards. On top of that, BIAP was always expecting a nighttime rocket attack, and no one wanted to be blitzed when it happened.

Pornography, on the other hand, was verboten because the Powers That Be were concerned that it would insult the Muslim population. This, even after many American soldiers caught Iraqi men viewing male porn on their computers. Whatever trips your trigger...

Getting back to the care package. I rip open the box with 20 pairs of eyes anticipating the treasures within. On top: a Playboy magazine!

Oh, but of course! Some role model I'm turning out to be. Nothing like having 2 quarts of adrenaline dumped into your bloodstream. I frantically stuff the unclean thing back into the box, down the side. Those ladies at work will get me court-martialed yet!!

The next item is a huge jar of Gatorade. Just what I need to add to my already burgeoning supply of hydration drinks. Apparently, most Americans believe that the U.S. military refuses to provide water for their soldiers, or that we're stuck in a remake of the movie, "The Flight of the Phoenix." Endless sand dunes and only camels to keep us company.

In keeping with my female co-workers' sense of "fun", the next object is GI Joe Barbie, complete with fatigues, combat boots and an M-16. One large chuckle from the Peanut Gallery. I try to laugh off the doll; I tell the team that I plan on giving her to the daughter of the village mayor we're working with currently.

"Yeah, right, Major Ready", one of the soldiers teases me.

I place GI Joe Barbie on the bookcase in my quarters, fully intending to carry out my intention of finding her a home with a small Iraqi girl. The next morning, the doll is missing. Ha! Very funny!

I forget about the incident until about 2 weeks later, I receive an envelope from a PO Box in San Diego; the only problem is: I don't know anyone there. Inside is a ransom note made up entirely of letters cut from newspapers warning me that if I don't convince Colonel Herriot to grant a 3 day pass for everyone in the battalion, I would never see GI Joe Barbie again. Somebody has entirely too much time on his or her hands! I mean, I'd forgotten about the doll. And, it'll take a LOT more than that to get passes to Qatar.

A few weeks later, I get another envelope, this one postmarked in Geneva, Switzerland. Inside, there is no ransom note, only a dozen strands of fake blonde hair. Like you would find on a Barbie Doll. A

G.I. Joe Barbie Doll.

We need to get moving on buying satellite dishes and television sets for these troops. Or the Airport really needs a bowling alley!

Needless to say, I still did not pester the Colonel about the Qatar passes, a decision which would prove disastrous 3 days later. I'm working on one of the endless stream of reports that need to be typed up, when I notice an email alert.

It's from KidnapperOfGIJoeBarbieInIraq@yahoo.com. There's an attachment. On my screen is a photo of GI Joe Barbie. She's naked except for her combat boots and a blindfold. Glued to her mouth is a crude gag made from a tiny black ball and a strip of cloth. And, you guessed it, she's been hogtied.

By this time, after weeks of this, my sense of humor has deserted me. I'm extremely stressed out. This stupid report I'm working on is overdue, and I'm being verbally slapped by my superiors on an hourly basis.

So, I have a psychotic episode.

I get up from my desk, stomp out into the hallway, which overlooks a courtyard within the Crack House complex, and yell at the top of my lungs: "I don't want fucking GI Joe Barbie! You can keep her!!"

It's then that I realize the windows over the courtyard are open, and there are a half dozen female soldiers sitting together, cleaning their weapons. Staring up at me. So perfect.

Trying to recoup my dignity, I wave to the still gawking members of the fairer sex, and call out: "Hello! How are you?"

War is Hell; Wish You Were Here

I'm on the phone with one of my sisters back in the States. Each one of us is allowed to use the military cell phone for twenty minutes' duration. We use calling cards sent to us in "care packages" from family, friends, or kind strangers. It's a lot better than waiting for mail, and has more immediacy than email. She's filling me in on how things are with my parents, etc. For a few minutes, I can forget about Iraq. But, not for long. Once again, I hear muffled explosions, this time mixed with rifle fire. A lot of rifle fire. I cut her off in mid-sentence.

"I think we're under attack."

"What did you say?"

"I said I think we're under attack."

My sister is completely blown away that she's talking to me while my life expectancy could be measured in seconds.

"John, for God's sake, get off the phone! Take cover!" she screams from halfway around the world. She hangs up.

You'd think bin Laden's right on my tail.

I can still hear the fighting in the distance; thankfully, it doesn't appear to be anywhere near us. It's at this time that I realize the cell phone battery is dead, and I can't find my charger. It's going to be a while before I can call her back and tell her the coast is clear, and not to worry.

In the meantime, she calls every living relative on the Eastern seaboard and informs them, in no uncertain terms, that I'm in a fire-fight, and that I'll be going out in a blaze of glory very soon.

As it turns out, we're not under attack. Some of the soldiers are in the break room watching Band of Brothers on their DVD player.

Christmas in Baghdad.
Photo courtesy John Ready

Cheesy furniture at Saddam's Al Faw Palace
Photo courtesy of Amy Polsinelli

Our illegal mascot, Asia
Photo courtesy John Ready

Fun with Photoshop.
Photo courtesy John Ready

Iraqi schoolgirl
Photo courtesy Amy Polsinelli

Operation Rosebud
Photo courtesy John Ready

Our commander, doing what he hated the most
Photo courtesy John Ready

Reunion at Saranac Brewing Company. 2012
Photo courtesy John Ready

Poop can fly, baby!
Photo courtesy John Ready

"Park your car, Sir?" Aftermath of an IED attack on MSR Tampa
Photo courtesy John Ready

In Iraq with Kuwaiti Border Guards after invasion.
Photo courtesy John Ready

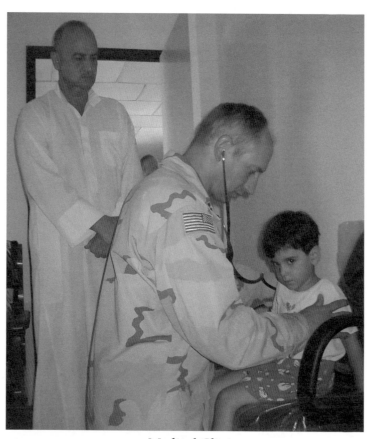

Medical Clinic
Photo courtesy John Ready

Batman chowing down
Photo courtesy John Ready

Babysitting in Baghdad
Photo courtesy John Ready

Iraqi child
Photo courtesy John Ready

SGT Amy gets her 15 minutes
Photo courtesy John Ready

The Crack House, our home and office.
Photo courtesy John Ready

Something Old, Something New, Something Borrowed, Something Blew Up

We had done a number of projects in the village of Chaldea, outside the Airport. Because of this, we had established a very good rapport with the residents, so much so that we were constantly invited for dinner and other events.

One weekend, we were invited to a wedding. Now, Iraqi and American nuptials are pretty much the same; with two glaring differences:

No alcohol. None.

Here in the States, we throw rice. In the Middle East, rice is too precious, so instead the celebrants fire AK-47's into the air.

This tradition makes American soldiers nervous. A GI is trained from the first day in the military that the sound of gunfire not emanating from his or her location is bad news. His first instinct is to drop into the prone and shoot back. Keeping this in mind, I spoke to the Force Protection Officer, a captain who was in charge of securing the airport perimeter. His men were the first line of defense for our base; if they over-reacted when they heard celebratory gunfire, they could bring a lot of firepower down on us. I didn't want to leave anything to chance.

"We're invited to a wedding in Chaldea", I told him. "Please let your troops know that if they hear AK-47 fire coming from there, it's only in celebration."

He assured me that he would notify everyone on the perimeter. My New Best Buddy reminded me that the Rules of Engagement (ROE) dictated hostile fire had to be confirmed before anyone unleashed an arsenal of weaponry.

Soon, we arrived at the groom's home in the village. I would have been content with the Captain's assurances but the problem is, well, I'm paranoid. Not just "Regular Paranoid", but "Roswell Paranoid". I believe the next level up is "New World Order Paranoid", but I'm not there. Yet.

I climbed back into the HUMVEE and called the captain on the radio. "Hey, remember me? I'm the guy who talked to you about fifteen minutes ago. Uh, I just wanted to make sure that we're on the same sheet of music. I mean, we have an understanding, right, Chief?" I could tell that he was getting annoyed with me. He reiterated that we were all on the same team.

Not exactly, I thought. He's inside The Wire, we're out: not exactly what I would call a "team".

Iraqi groom: "I do."

Iraqi bride: "I do."

Oh, shit! Here it comes!!

BUP-BUP-BUP-BUP-BUP-BUP-BUP!!!

Not to beat a dead horse, but why can't they just have a Dollar Dance?

What Are You Wearing?

Our uniforms were called Desert Camouflage Uniforms (DCUs). They were a pattern of sand, pale green and brown. They did a fair job of keeping us from being spotted in a desert environment. I don't have faith in the camouflage pattern the Army uses now: Digital Grey. Where'd they think that would work, the Moon? At least they got the Woodland pattern right: green, black, brown, and tan.

The problem was, the Army didn't have enough body armor in the DCU pattern. Therefore, we were forced to wear ballistic vests called IBA (Interceptor Body Armor) that were colored-you guessed it-Woodland Camouflage.

Tell me this is not a government operation....

If the purpose of using DCUs was to actually prevent an enemy from spotting soldiers in the desert, then having dark colored vests gave them something to aim at. It's just another example of the supply screw-ups that marked Operation Iraqi Freedom. And believe me, that was just the beginning.

Upon arrival at BIAP, things were pretty Spartan: there were no shower or laundry facilities. We had to "make do." A shower was accomplished by a upending a 5-gallon plastic water can over yourself, only dribbling enough to get you wet. Then, you applied soap (hopefully) and lathered up. Then you poured water over yourself, again just enough to rinse.

Doing laundry consisted of filling a shallow plastic tub with water, just enough to immerse your dirty clothing, add soap of some kind and drain the water out of the garments by twisting the cloth.

After a few weeks, some enterprising Iraqi's set up laundry operations. We gave our dirty clothing to our translator in marked plastic bags, and then he would get it to the laundry. A few days later, the clean uniforms would be returned, cleaned and pressed. There were a couple of problems, though.

The first was that the uniforms smelled faintly of kerosene. OK, if that's what it took to get them clean, then so be it. I'm just glad I never took up smoking.

The second issue is that we often got back the wrong clothing, even though they left us in bags clearly marked. The labels inside the uniforms were also marked with our names and units. The shirts had our nametags, also.
Sooooo, what the hell happened?

After a lot of yelling and threatening to fire the drycleaner, this problem was eventually ironed out. No pun intended.

The "Hey, Here We Are" ballistic vests we were issued had pockets in the front and back where the SAPI (Small Arms Protective Inserts) plates were placed. These were made of hardened ceramic composite and were engineered to stop rifle bullets. It saved at least one of my troop's lives.

For the first four months of our deployment, our CA battalion was only issued enough plates to wear in the front of our vests. I told our parent CA brigade's supply officer that this was a disaster waiting to happen.

"Well, just make sure you don't run away from the enemy!"

Yuk Yuk!

Oxygen Thief!

In addition to the vest, each of us had a detachable groin protector. If we'd had enough of them, I would have worn three, more for psychological than physical protection from the Mother of All Wounds. Everybody was afraid of that one.

I remember the temperature that summer reaching 140 degrees. But that's when I stopped checking. That would have been bad if we were just wearing the uniform. Add the Kevlar helmet (4 lbs), IBA (12-15), ammo, water and rations, and you're tooling around the desert or Downtown Baghdad with at least fifty pounds.

Did I mention it was a dry heat? I've worn gear that heavy in humid weather at Fort Polk, LA and even Fort Drum, NY. In that environment, if a troop stops sweating, robbing his body of its mechanism of cooling itself, his buddies can spot this and render aid. Replace the fluids lost before the onset of heat exhaustion, or worse, heat stroke.

In the Middle East, the climate is generally arid. Your sweat evaporates almost right away. It's harder for your comrades to notice you're in danger of overheating. That happened to me twice. I don't do well in the heat. The times I went on local purchase excursions in Downtown Baghdad are glaring testaments to that.

If you want a good indication of how oppressive the heat is in Iraq:

Preheat your oven to 500 degrees. Wear multiple layers of clothing, preferably a heavy snowmobile suit. Place a saucepan on your head Open the oven door and try to stick your body in as far as you can. If you feel like you just can't take it any more, don't quit. Maybe you could have a friend who's a real jerk block you from escaping. Now, you have somewhat of an idea of what our soldiers have to endure in that climate all of the time.

If I end up in Hell, I'll ask for a blanket.

Headache. Stomach is doing calisthenics, and I feel like I gotta puke. Except I haven't eaten breakfast. Eating involves movement, which would make me even hotter and miserable. I guzzle water from my canteen, a piece of military gear made by the lowest bidder that adds a polystyrene aftertaste to its contents.

Now, I REALLY want to puke!

It's High Noon on Karada Street, one of the shopping districts in Baghdad. I'm standing on a sidewalk in front of one of the dozens of appliance stores. Three of my soldiers are inside, negotiating with the proprietor in order to get the best price for The Greatest Invention in the World: air conditioners. Because of the wildly fluctuating exchange rate between the Iraqi Dinar and the US Dollar, it's important to try and get the most bang for the buck.

Don't say bang...

They're certainly taking their sweet ass time. I've never enjoyed shopping, and doing it in a combat zone while wearing all this extra poundage is really unpleasant. Plus there's always the possibility of getting attacked. Even though it's the role of Civil Affairs to procure supplies off the local economy, sitting in a concrete canyon like this is asking for trouble. Being primarily an Infantry officer, I have a healthy disdain for staying in one spot for any length of time. It appears that I'm the only one who's concerned. Maybe the heat is getting to me.

An Iraqi woman scuttles up to me in a black abaya, a garment that covers everything but her feet and hands. Her hair is under a veil called a hijab; only her weather-beaten face is exposed. It's impossible to discern her age.

She is selling hand fans. The woman obviously hasn't heard the latest rumor circulating among the Iraqi population: American soldiers are able to withstand the oppressive heat because they are equipped with air-conditioned helmets and underwear.

I mean we put men on the moon, right? Is it too much of a Giant Leap to have air- conditioned helmets and underwear?

I'm here to tell you we did NOT have those..

The woman holds up the hand fans and speaks urgently the only English she knows:

"Mistah! Mistah! Baby! Baby!

Oh great! She's trying to shame me into buying one of her fans. After all, this is her only livelihood. Can't blame her for trying.

Excessive heat and imminent danger bring out the wiseass in me. I just don't give a shit who I offend or piss off.

"You told me you weren't looking for a relationship! You said you were on the pill!"

The fans drop to her sides. She stares at me, shocked. I doubt she understands my wisecracks. She probably just wasn't expecting me to jabber at her in English while buying a stupid hand fan. This crazy American has been driven mad by the heat.

He probably has.

I'm done messing with her. I hand her a dollar bill. She moves to give me one of her fans, but I gently push her hand back.

She's going to need that more than me, I say to myself. Turns out I was wrong.

The negotiating inside the store has been going on far too long. What the Hell is taking so long? Our 6 HUMVEE'S are big, fat targets out here between the tall buildings. I begin to have visions of men pointing AK-47 rifles and Rocket Propelled Grenade launchers at us from every rooftop, window and doorway.

I'm starting to panic, because all I want to do, my only wish, my sole purpose in life at this moment is to have all this gear taken off me. If it isn't soon, it's going to drive me insane.

I get my wish.

My vision is blurred. I suddenly feel very tired. My legs are like rubber and now I'm really nauseous. I stumble to the shop entrance, intent on seeking shade and my troops who are obviously procrastinating and causing me all this discomfort on purpose.

KLUNK!!!

My Kevlar helmet bumps into something. It's the concrete sidewalk. I'm lying flat on my face.

How did I get here?

I can feel hands turning me over onto my back. My vest, helmet and shirt are removed, just like I'd wanted. I feel sharp pains on the backs of both hands. I try to lift my head to see what's up.

"Whoa! Go easy, Major. Just lay back. We're running you a couple of IV'S. You're pretty dehydrated." It's the medic from the MP platoon providing our convoy escort.

I tell him I drank a lot of water; I don't understand how I've gone down for the count from heat exhaustion. He asks me if I've eaten anything today, and I tell him that I didn't.

"Congratulations, Sir. You didn't take in any electrolytes, and you flushed the ones you did have out of your body by drinking all that water. Don't worry, Sir. You'll feel better later."

Twelve hours and nine IV bags later. And this happens to me after I'm basically standing around. I can't imagine how the combat troops are doing when they're running around kicking in doors and humping rucksacks in this oven.

And they call this the Cradle of Civilization!

Oh, by the way: If anybody reading this knows a soldier named Butler who was deployed to Baghdad in the Summer of 2003, I have his underwear.

Looking for Mr. Good Bar-biturate

"The church is near but the road is icy, the tavern is far away, but I will walk carefully."

-Russian Proverb

"This is not war; it's detox."

-Latrine graffiti at Baghdad International Airport

While we were deployed to the Middle East, alcohol consumption was strictly forbidden. We were considered "guests" in Kuwait and Iraq, both predominately Muslim countries. The big fear of the Command was that drunken servicemen and women would offend the strict Muslims in our host countries.

Now, my take on this is that, if you send young men and women into harm's way, you should allow them to drink some freaking alcohol once in a while.

On the other hand, the FOB was always expecting a catastrophic rocket attack, which was a very real threat, and you never knew when it would come. It was always hanging over our heads, and nobody wanted to be three sheets to the wind when it happened.

So, unfortunately, it was a good policy.

I'm riding in the HUMVEE, on my way to another boring meeting. My driver is doing his best to negotiate the countless potholes in the road to DIVARTY Headquarters, and still maintain a good clip. We're running late for the meeting, and one thing the Army hates is an officer being late for a meeting.

The vehicle slows and I'm jerked from my stupor; there's a 5-ton truck stopped dead in the road in front of us.

"Oh, come on! Not now!" I yell out loud. This is going to make me late for the meeting. Everyone will stare at me as I walk into the TOC;

everyone, of course, but the DIVARTY Commander, who will probably bark at me, venom dripping from his jaws.

I see three soldiers at the back of the truck, hurriedly picking up cardboard boxes that have fallen from the truck bed, and heaving them back in. The boxes are stenciled in red with one long word:

BUDWEISER

Alcohol! Numbing agent. Escape.

It doesn't say that, of course; those were the words flashing like a neon sign in my mind. I can't believe they are allowing booze here; everybody here has been "jonesing" for it, and now it's Christmas! How this is allowed in a Muslim country is beyond me, but I'm ecstatic.

"Let's stop and help them!" I tell my driver.

"But, Sir, you'll be late for the meeting."

"Fuck the meeting! I yell. Maybe, they'll let us have some for helping to secure the truck!"

I jump from the HUMVEE, and stride authoritatively up to the soldiers.

"Need some help?" Please?

One of the poor troops looks up and his eyes lock onto the Major's oak leaf on my collar. He snaps to the position of attention.

"Um, sure, Sir. I mean, we're almost done, Sir."

"No problem, Sergeant!" I say helpfully. "We can't move around you anyway, where the truck is stopped."

"O-OK, Sir", the young man stammers. He looks totally bewildered and freaked out: His perception of Majors is that they are always busy attending meetings. They NEVER stop to help out lower-ranking troops with such menial tasks as rousting spilled cases of non-alcoholic beer.

Because that's what in the truck's cargo: Near beer. Less than 1% alcohol by volume. It says so on the label, which was illegible until I was up close.

NO BUZZ

LIKE TAKING A SHOWER WITH A RAINCOAT ON

A FERRARI WITH A YUGO ENGINE

"Shit!" I say out loud. "I should have known it was too good to be true!"

I run back to my vehicle, totally pissed.

"Get going!" I grumble. "I'm gonna be late! Go around these guys!"

"My God, you're fickle," I hear my driver mutter under his breath.

My hopes are dashed. I'd convinced myself I was finally going to relax with a cold one at night. The sergeant looks a little upset, too; he had a great story in his grasp of how a Major helped him and his soldiers load a truck.

I'm late for my meeting.

Some troops try, in vain, to catch a buzz by telling their medics or physician assistants that they've hurt their backs lifting heavy objects. The medics prescribe them Valium. Then, they guzzle a near beer and try and pretend it's the real deal.

"Wait, I think I feel it! Wait! Wait!"

"Oh, yeah, that's good!"

In the PX (Post Exchange), the military supermarket, sit cases upon cases of Non-alcoholic beer. It's just not the same as REAL alcohol, forcing troops to become desperate and make their own. Disaster.

I get a call on my cell phone. It's the Division Personnel (G1) section: I've been selected to be an Investigating Officer regarding an incident with two of their young sergeants. The officer conducting the investigation usually is field grade in rank, which I was, and outside of the their unit, in order to insure impartiality. G1 somehow got it in their head that I didn't have enough paperwork to do.

I arrive at the unit requesting the investigation, in order to find out what crime the two NCOs allegedly committed. Turns out these two guys were making their own hooch.

Now, I know that there was a ban on alcohol in the area of operations. And all good officers and NCOs are supposed to uphold General Order Number One. But, I'd witnessed a lot of soldiers, officers and NCOs alike, who were getting drunk as lords just about every night. And I'm supposed to be part of getting these two young soldiers punished, probably busted in rank?

But, mine is not to reason why...

"Sir, during an inspection of their quarters, we found a half-empty carton of pineapple juice with pieces of bread stuck inside."

Hmm, the fermentation process. It's that easy?

For some reason, this intrigues me. I suddenly take an interest in the case.

"Sir, this is a clear violation of General Order Num-"

"Hold on a second! Back up! How many pieces of bread did you say? How much pineapple juice has to be in the carton?"

The World Through My Window

I'm stuck in my office. At least I've got CNN on the satellite TV.

I've got all these reports to write; they're due by 1700. It's amazing how slowly time seems to crawl here, except when you have a deadline and some Brass breathing down your neck.

Dust is blowing through a small crack in The Window. It settles on my desk, my laptop, even in my coffee. I've put up with it for 4 months so far; I'm way past the point of caring. Even the rats are starting to look cute.

An explosion in the distance.

And another.

The deep, hollow pops of a machine gun invade my lethargy. I start violently and glance out The Window, past the neat rows of choppers parked on the runway apron.

My eyes lock onto 2 clouds of smoke to the North. They're not like the usual clouds marking the ever-present burn pits; these are oily, angry plumes reaching into the sky.

Somebody just got hit. Got hit bad.

One of the radios comes to life. It's the one set to the Force Protection net, base security.

"Steel Main!! Steel Main!! Troops in contact! Request immediate MEDEVAC and QRF, over!"

Steel Main: "Roger. Last calling station: say call sign and grid, over."

Pacesetter 3 Lima:
"This is Pacesetter 3 Lima! My grid is Mike Bravo 4306 8979!

We're hit! Get us to a hospital! "

Steel Main: "Roger. Calm down! I copy grid Mike Bravo 4306 8979. How many PAX? "

Pacesetter 3 Lima: "I have 2 wounded and 1 KIA! One has a sucking chest wound and shrap metal in the face and arms. Medic has a chest tube in but he's bleeding quick!"
I got another guy's taken a round in the chest, up high near the arteries, and a through and through in the left forearm!

Unknown: "Steel Main, Steel Main. This is November 16 Romeo, radio check, over."

Steel Main: "Stay off the radio! We have troops in contact!"

November 16 Romeo: "Say again, Steel Main. I didn't cop-"

Oh, you ass clown! Can't you hear? He's got two Priority MEDE-VAC'S! God, please get those birds out there before it's too late.

Steel Main: "All stations this net! All stations this net! Wait out! Clear this net!!!!"

BREAK!   BREAK!   BREAK!

"Copy that, Pacesetter. MEDEVAC is alerted. Dust Off 15 is on 128.6. Make contact with her on that freak but continue to monitor this channel for further instructions."

Almost simultaneously, another radio, this one tuned to Baghdad Tower, adds its own drama. I can still hear the calm, soothing Kiwi voices of the Royal Australian Air Force controllers.

Tower: "Roger that, Dustoff 15! Fly runway heading, maintain 500 feet. You are cleared to the Oscar Beacon, break out to the North-Northwest, heading Three Zero Zero."

Dustoff 15: "Copy that, Tower! Runway heading to Oscar, turn heading Three Zero Zero."

There is a determination in her voice that leads me to believe the two WIAs have a chance.

Two of the Blackhawks taxi to the runway. They sit there, poised, ready for takeoff. They lurch upward, hovering briefly, like a couple of wasps. Their noses dip suddenly and they bank to the North, to the dark clouds rising from the city of Abu Ghraib. I can just barely make out the symbol painted on the underside of one of the choppers before they disappear into 2 black specks: red cross on a white background. Medevac, in military jargon. Air ambulance. The other is a gunship, traveling along for protection. The insurgents think nothing of firing at medical choppers. They don't honor the Geneva Convention or the Law of Land Warfare. But that's a topic of a much larger debate.

Dustoff 15: "Pacesetter 3 Lima, Dustoff is inbound. How is your LZ (Landing Zone) marked?"

Pacesetter 3 Lima: "Dustoff, The LZ is not secure! Be advised, we are still taking small arms fire at this time!"

There's a long pause. The radio is silent. The kind of silence you would encounter, perhaps, after a fart in church.

Then, the MEDEVAC pilot finally speaks. She doesn't say much, and it's not in a loud voice; it's how she says it that makes me turn cold in 130-degree heat.

Dustoff 15: "WELL, UNLESS YOU WANT THOSE KIDS TO DIE, I SUGGEST YOU FIND ME SOMEPLACE TO LAND, 'CUZ I'M ONLY ABOUT 2 MINUTES OUT."

Her tone lets everybody know there's NO room for discussion: She doesn't want to hear or see a single bullet when she lands.

It has the desired effect:

Steel Main: "Pacesetter 3 Lima, Dustoff 15, the QRF inform me that they are at the ambush site."

And shortly thereafter:

Pacesetter 3 Lima: "Dustoff, my LZ is now secure!"

Dustoff 15: "That's more like it, gentlemen!"

I love it when she takes charge...

Watching, waiting, wondering what happened and who got it. Is it someone I know? Maybe somebody I know from the fuel point? The dining facility? Who knows?

God, it better not be my guys! Are they out there today?

I check the Mission Board, frantically noting the grid coordinates and head to the big map on the wall. I let my breath out slowly. No, that's not where they went today.

An hour crawls by with no word about who got hit. Suddenly, CNN starts splashing images that seem eerily familiar to me: it's the highway running along the South side of Abu Ghraib. Dark clouds of smoke pouring from blazing vehicles. Blackhawk helicopters are parked off to one side.

The reporter says there was an IED (Improvised Explosive Device) ambush. Then the insurgents fired up the convoy with AK-47's just to prove they are dicks. A supply convoy from LOG BASE SEITZ, north of the airport. I used to go meetings at that base when we first got here. It probably was somebody I know.

This is surreal. People watching CNN back home have the same information I have.

I hear it over here, and it comes out up there. Bizarre!

I feel like a spectator to someone else's war, insulated by distance.

I won't feel insulated much longer.

Seeing the Elephant

"The best laid schemes o' mice an' men/Gang aft a-gley," (shit happens)

– Robert Burns, Ode To A Mouse

It's been said that every soldier hopes to go to war in his or her lifetime. After years of training for just such an event, there is a deep desire to prove oneself. The soldier doesn't necessarily want to kill or maim (unlike the Trained Killer), but he anticipates the question from his grandchild: "What did you do during the war, Grandpa?" He doesn't want to answer that he sat on the sidelines during such a monumental world event. He's afraid of not doing his part.

There's a very famous story of the farmer who'd heard that the circus was coming to a nearby town. Setting out the following morning in his wagon, the farmer hoped to see this exotic creature. At the nearby railroad crossing, a grove of trees blocked his vision, but the farmer urged his horse into the crossing anyway. At that same moment the circus train, with the elephant in the first car, sped on by. The resulting collision smashed the wagon, killed the horse, and laid the farmer out cold.

The circus train passed on as though nothing had happened. Regaining consciousness, the farmer saw the destruction and said dryly, "Well, at least I've seen the elephant."

The first week in July 2003 was when we saw our herd of elephants. On the first day of the month, a well-regarded NCO assigned to the CACOM, First Sergeant Chris Langtry, died on MSR Tampa south of Baghdad. That was the first crack in the veneer that was our illusion of safety.

He had supposedly been killed in a vehicle rollover accident, but soon the rumors began to circulate that this was not the case. First, it was an accident, then an accident followed by an attack by an angry mob. He died as a result of being crushed to by the vehicle's heavy load. Then we heard he'd been shot.

What's significant about this misinformation is that everyone knew that Chris was being sent into harm's way on a weekly basis. He constantly had to travel back and forth from Baghdad to Kuwait, through nearly 400 miles of hostile territory. His superiors had screwed up their logistics operation, and they were making he and another soldier drive all that way to fix it.

I read later that First Sergeant Langtry had complained to his wife by email that he was having to perform this almost impossible job without adequate convoy security. Whether or not his death was by accident or insurgent attack, it was just a foregone conclusion.

I had worked with him while we were in Kuwait. He was the consummate professional, and it was obvious that he only had the interests of his soldiers in the forefront of his mind. I learned of his death while attending a nightly briefing at DIVARTY; it was such a shock, the news made me buckle at the knees.

Since June, there had been steady reports of soldiers being killed and wounded; the insurgency was gearing up, but it was like watching somebody else's war. Chris' death was the first casualty that put a face on that war.

The commander of our higher CA brigade, Colonel Merritt, began holding mandatory meetings for his battalion commanders at 1800 hours every night. They were held at the Puzzle Palace, the opulent building that had once been the living quarters for Iraq's military elite. Most of the brigade leadership was headquartered in the Green Zone, but there were others in Baghdad that were miles away, like ours and the 490th Civil Affairs Battalion. To attend the meetings, Colonel Herriot had to take the Baghdad Airport Road, or ROUTE IRISH.

The colonel and Team Testosterone head out to the commanders' meeting in two HUMVEES. An hour later, the field telephone rings in the TOC. On the line is a staff officer at the brigade headquarters downtown. The room turns dark and my heart stops, as he notifies me that the convoy has been hit with an IED on ROUTE IRISH. SFC

Morrissey is WIA (Wounded in Action).

Oh my God… The news hits me like a ton of bricks. Somehow, I gather my wits, and begin taking down the details and writing reports. I'm grateful that there's work to be done: it'll keep my head clear and allow me to take charge. Because right now, I'd like nothing better than to bask in denial and turn back the clock. Anything that would change the awful truth that one of the lives entrusted to me has been altered forever.

The incident details poured in. The driver of the lead HUMVEE had just been on ROUTE IRISH a couple of hours before. As the two vehicles left the main gate, he spotted a shiny metal can near the right shoulder. A warning light had come on inside his brain:

THAT WASN'T THERE BEFORE!

Instinctively, he swerved toward the left side of the highway and stepped on the accelerator, praying that the trail HUMVEE would follow. There was no time to call out a warning on the radio, so he resorted to non-verbal communication. It worked, and Big D, the driver of the second vehicle, swerved and floored it in kind. This simple maneuver was one of the factors in saving Morrissey's life. Even though he was sitting in the cargo area, guarding the convoy's rear, the IED was just far enough away to spare him the full force of the blast.

As it was, SFC Morrissey suffered shrapnel wounds in all four extremities. One of his legs was fractured, also. Another factor that had spared his life was the SAPI plate in his ballistic vest. Colonel ordered the team to speed about a quarter mile down ROUTE IRISH before they pulled over to work on the wounded sergeant. Abbas, our translator, grabbed Morrissey's rifle and provided security. When Colonel Herriot finally reached the Puzzle Palace, Colonel Merritt stalked up, and asked, "Colonel Herriot! What were you doing on that road?"

Herriot turned to him and snarled, "I was going to your fucking meeting, Sir!"

The general commanding the Civil Affairs troops in Baghdad,

Mad Cow, criticized Colonel Herriot for not driving far enough away from the ambush site before stopping to render aid to Morrissey. Our commander protested that our man was losing blood and in danger of going into shock. The general replied: "People can bleed for quite a while before they require medical attention."

Right, and besides that Mrs. Lincoln, how was the play?

I need to point out that Mad Cow was not a medical doctor, or any kind of doctor for that matter. Who knows; maybe he got a degree from the University of Baghdad....

All this because a commander wanted to meet face-to-face with his subordinates, when a conference call would have been the smarter course of action.

Our detachment, already low on personnel, now had a dilemma: whenever a team went on a mission, they had to adhere to the force protection guidelines in effect for that day. There were to be a minimum of two vehicles on any travel outside the wire. Each HUMVEE needed to have three long guns (M-16's, automatic weapons, etc.). With SFC Morrissey out of action, we needed to plug replacements into the void.

The replacement pool consisted solely of SFC Wilkes and I. The Trained Killer, who was responsible for making sure the missions were staffed, didn't consider Wilkes to be sufficiently bad-ass, so he deliberately kept her back at the Crack House. I volunteered to go along as security on any missions, but the Trained Killer told me that wasn't necessary. I thought to protest and overrule him, but let it go. This set the stage for disaster.

Our troops were scheduled to meet with a well-drilling contractor in a village with the unlikely name of "Block 16". The moniker was given to this small settlement during the 1917 British occupation. The area including this village had a serious water shortage due to the irrigation system being in a terrible state of disrepair. SSG Richardson, SGT Amy, SGT Richfield, and their interpreter, Sayyid, met with him to contract for drilling water wells.

They took one vehicle.

Unknown to us, insurgents had been watching our team for the past month, ever since we had surveyed the landowners on the airport's western perimeter, with the eventual goal of evicting them. This area included Block 16.

Another call on the telephone: it's the same staff officer who'd broken the news about Morrissey. He tells me that one of our soldiers has been wounded. Puzzled, I start to remind him that he's already told me about Morrissey. Then, it hits home.

It's happening again.

Just like two days before, the walls close in on me. My breathing is shallow, and I can hear the blood rushing in my brain. The Voice tells me that SGT Richfield has been wounded.

This time, I cannot keep the panic from overtaking me. On autopilot, I frantically make telephone and radio calls, trying to find out exactly what happened, after having had my heart torn out and thrown to the floor.

The Force Protection Officer from 1AD filled me in on the details. The team had left the contractor's home, and was turning onto the paved road leading back to BIAP. A red sedan drove up behind them. Someone inside opened up with an AK-47, spraying the HUMVEE with bullets.

The insurgents obviously saw a single HUMVEE as an easy target. If I'd insisted that I go along with SFC Wilkes, we could have had two vehicles. Instead, I let it slide.

SGT Richfield took a round in the left ankle. He was still able to steer the vehicle, even though he was losing blood and consciousness. SSG Richardson was in the front passenger seat, and was unable to return fire. Sayyid wasn't able to fasten his seatbelt in time. When the HUMVEE sped up, the motion launched him out the side. He hit his head on a stone and was knocked unconscious.

SGT Amy turned in her seat, and began laying down suppressive fire to keep the ambushers' heads down. The vehicle limped toward the base, and was intercepted by a Marine convoy. The Leathernecks stabilized Richfield, and stormed back into Block 16 to rescue Sayyid. The Iraqi had been a POW for eight years during the Iran-Iraq War decades earlier. Today was his first, and last day, on the job. The next week, we went to his house to see how he was mending. His wife went ballistic, and screamed for us to leave. Can't say I blamed her.

It had finally happened: we'd been bloodied. Our mission went from solely humanitarian in nature, to one of self-preservation. It was debatable about whether or not we were ever safe before this, but now there was no doubt. Iraq was a room in total darkness, filled with sharp, nasty objects.

We'd lost our innocence.

I'm OK, You Need Help

Son of a bitch, my head hurts!

I'm in the throes of the Mother of All Sinus Infections. This condition has plagued me my entire life, but this one takes the cake. My eyes feel like they are on fire, there's a nasty taste in my mouth, and I'm nauseous. I've spent most of the year trying to avoid rockets. Today, I want one of them to glide up my right nostril and end my misery.

The omnipresent Iraqi sand, which has the consistency of talcum powder, is the culprit. You figure that all that sand has been swirling around for millions of years, the particles colliding with each other over and over. Eventually, that shit's going to penetrate tightly woven fabrics, foul weapons, and remove the lining of my sinus cavities. Anything used to make bricks shouldn't be inside you. (Six years from now, I'll undergo surgery to remove dozens of polyps from my inside my noggin, growths which were probably caused by the dust. The doctor jokes that he's found everything but Jimmy Hoffa and a toy Hess truck in there.)

During the rainy season, the standing water mixes with the dust, coating highways with an impossible slick that rivals black ice back in Central New York, causing vehicles to slide off the road and into each other.

It turns out Iraq has a weapon of mass destruction after all.

I decide to throw in the towel and seek out a doctor. There's a medical clinic close to our building, so I shuffle over, seeking relief. Their colonel, an Ear, Nose and Throat Specialist in private practice back home, hands me a small bottle of Azithromycin. He tells me to follow the dosage carefully, and come back in two days. I'm so out of it, I don't hear him; all I can do is stare at the elixir that will take away the pain.

Two days later, the doc asks me how I'm feeling.

"Sir, I feel great! That stuff worked like a charm! I chugged it right after you gave it to me."

His eyes widen. "Tell me you didn't drink the entire bottle!"

Sheepishly, I ask, "You mean I wasn't supposed to?"

"No, Major! Now get over to the chow hall and grab as much yogurt as you can carry back. You just killed all the bacteria in your body, even the good kind, you know, for proper digestion.

And the next time we meet, we'll go over the "doctor-patient thing" one more time."

After the week in July when Morrissey and Richfield were wounded, the three days we got bloodied and lost our innocence, the higher-ups realized that we needed an intervention. We were ordered to stand down and cease operations. This is normal procedure when a unit has a high casualty rate; in our case it was 10%.

We were also ordered to undergo counseling, as by this point, we were dangerously close to being combat ineffective. With the twin bombshells that were dropped on us fresh in our minds, our superiors had serious concerns that we would lose our focus and make dire mistakes. In my case, those concerns were justified, and I wasn't even going outside the wire like the rest of them.

I had allowed myself to become complacent, finally giving in and believing the hype that the Iraqis would continue to welcome us into their homeland. My premonitions of the security situation going to Hell were shoved into my back pocket. So, when the shit hit the fan, the fan was not prepared. After that terrible week, it seemed every decision I had to make contained potential for disaster. My mind rode a pendulum that moved from complacency and confidence on one end, to self-doubt and paranoia on the other.

In contemporary military slang, I was a whiny bitch.

The Army Combat Stress Team met with us as a team, and then

each of us individually. When my time on the therapy couch came, I sat with the psychologist outside under a lean-to near the Crack House. The psychologist, a major same as myself, began our session by relating her experiences and incidents to mine. She was the team commander. I listened as we watched a huge C-5A Galaxy start its takeoff roll on the nearest runway.

Man, I'd give anything to be on that bird right now! I wonder if the Air Force checks for stowaways.

"Now, I know exactly where you're at, mentally," she began. "I have to do my job and keep my sanity at the same time, along with worrying about being attacked while we travel from base to base. I acknowledge the fact that you're the Executive Officer, and you have all this responsibility and all these reports to write, and coordinating, etc.

"But, in order to keep doing all these things, effectively, you have to step away from it. Once a day, you just have to find a quiet place and think, meditate, pray, whatever you have to do. Right where we're sitting now is good. It's absolutely crucial that you find time for yourself. "

I was just beginning to let her words of wisdom sink in, when we were both startled by a distant bang, followed by a long, loud whooshing sound, and an even louder explosion. We stared at the C-5A climbing in a spiral above the airport. There was a smoke trail off to one side, punctuated at the end with a cloud of flames and white smoke. The insurgents had just fired a SAM at the Galaxy transport, and missed it by a couple hundred feet.

I lowered my eyes to her, and gave her my most ironic, fatalistic smile.

"Right, Doc."

We Could Talk About Current Events and Shit

Pre- and Post-Deployment Dating Fiascos

Dating sucks!

Especially right before you deploy. There's this girl I've met through one of those online dating sites. We'll call her Kristen.

Kristen is 35, single and never married. She's looking for a man. To make babies. She says her biological clock is ticking; my more cynical female friends tell me it's already tocked. That's the exact word they use, no lie.

She lives Downstate; somehow the Noguchi 500 Dating Compatibility Computer has screwed up and matched us, despite the fact that we live three and a half hours away, in good weather.

We begin seeing each other, anyway. More often than not, I drive down to her apartment. Sometimes we meet in Albany, and a few times she drives up to sleepy Oneida. We hit it off. We're both into spending money and wine tasting. I'm into an open-ended commitment as an officer in the Army Reserves, but not into recognizing an imminent relationship disaster. She isn't into taking her psychiatric medication. If it's true that love is blind, I must be her Seeing Eye dog.

Several months after our relationship, I got The Call: My Reserve unit was getting called up for deployment to Iraq. The Pentagon was mobilizing every Civil Affairs-qualified soldier in anticipation of the massive rebuilding that would be required after the ground war was over. As we've already discussed, calling up thousands of soldiers to rebuild a country doesn't really help if you don't have a plan. The Logic ran that planning would come later.

I'm still waiting.

Anyways, Kristen and I have The Big Talk when it's obvious

that I'm to be sent to Iraq. At the time, there's speculation that the deployment is to be a matter of months. Kristen tells me that she'll wait for me.

We have an entirely different conversation by phone much later, just after I'm told my battalion's tour will be extended into the following year.

Kristen: "I don't think I can wait that long!"

Me: "It's only a few more months. You told me that you would wait."

Kristen: "Yeah, but what if you don't come back?"

Me: "We're sorry, the number you have dialed is not in service. Please check the number and dial again, or contact the operator to find you another sucker. This is a recording!"

Holy shit! Are you freaking kidding me? I'm the one who's getting his ass shot at! Don't I count?

We agree to end the relationship. She's obviously given up; I figure I've dodged a bullet, and not one fired by an insurgent.

It's just as well; at one of the logistical bases that we frequent, I've met a female lieutenant. She's very pretty and has these beautiful blue eyes. That's all it takes; I am officially smitten with "Melissa."

One of my comrades volunteers to gather intelligence on her relationship status. According to his sources, she is single, only a few years younger than myself, and a fellow Reservist (which is important in that she will eventually go home, not be traipsing all over the globe with the Army, and therefore, be more apt to "settle down").

This woman is present at nearly every meeting that I have to attend. Suddenly, I start volunteering to go to more meetings, and even speak, which I've previously avoided like The Plague. I muster up the testosterone to chat her up. The colonel wants to know if I've caught something.

Well, kinda…

Me:" Hey, LT, my friend tells me you're in the Reserves just like me. Is this your first deployment, too?"

LT Melissa: "Yes, Sir!"

She calls me "Sir". So damned cute!

Me: (Moving in for the kill)" So, where's home?"

LT Melissa: "Rochester, Sir."

Me: "Oh, Rochester, Minnesota. I'll bet you have terrible winters just like we do in Syracuse."

LT Melissa: "Oh no, Sir. Rochester, New York. Actually, I live in a suburb called Brighton. And we get brutal lake effect snow, just like you folks in Syracuse."

This is too good to be true; I could drive back and forth to Rochester standing on my head!

She's beautiful and she lives only an hour away (when she's not at war).

Does her father own a liquor store, too? Or I have used up all three of my wishes?

Oh, yeah! We're gonna work this relationship!

    A couple of weeks later, I gleefully show up for one of our Commander's meetings, AKA Get To Know Her Better Talks. I spot her gliding toward me, with another officer who I don't recognize. A very large male.

They're holding hands. Shit!

Shit! Shit! Shit!

LT Melissa: "Hey, Sir! My boyfriend just proposed to me! I'm so happy! Look at my ring!"

Boyfriend? My HUMINT (Human Intelligence) source said nothing about a boyfriend! And now, we're at DEFCON 1 and he's a fiancé!

Me: "Congratulations, you two! My God! Look at the size of that rock!"

(I'm not thinking about her diamond, though; I'm referring to her fiancé, an Infantry Captain who obviously works out with very large objects, and who could probably crush my bones to powder, and turn my brain to water.)

Yep, good intelligence is SO hard to find. It keeps you from invading sovereign countries that you erroneously believe possess Weapons of Mass Destruction. It also keeps you from falling too hard, too fast for female officers in a combat zone, when you really should be focused on things that will help your troops do their job and stay safe.

A couple of weeks before we are scheduled to redeploy, a few of our soldiers figure that, since we now have an Internet Café all to ourselves, we should try our hand at online dating. About four of us single guys (and one married soldier who wants to be single) create dating profiles, hit the Launch button and settle down to await the flurry of single women who will be falling over themselves to meet single guys who are getting shot at in a combat zone.

And, we wait…and wait. Apparently, the novelty of dating combat vets has worn off back in the World.

Eventually, I win the online dating lottery and "meet" this woman just a couple of years younger who lives not as far Downstate as Kristen, and closer than Melissa. (I swear the Noguchi 500 creates a 50-mile exclusion zone around Oneida, wherein I am not allowed to date.) But, she is "single", and that's all that counts.

As the weeks go by, "Jessica" and I chat online and agree to meet once I get back home safe and sound.

Oh, yeah. Safe and sound. That.

The insurgency is in full swing; more attacks are occurring daily, and there is serious doubt about whether or not "Safe and Sound" will happen. The Boogie Man is lurking around the Airport, poised to lob mortars and rockets that will cut me down just before I am to leave to come home to America, civilization, my two sons, and Jessica. There are odds better than you could ever hope to get in Vegas that our convoy will be ambushed while on the 360-mile drive south to the relative sanctuary of Kuwait, and that I will die in a Last Stand on top of a sand dune. Don't get me wrong: I really, really want to entertain the idea of romance blooming in Oneonta on my return, but I need to keep my head in the game.

As it turns out, of course, we are spared any last ditch efforts by the Bad Guys to murder and maim us on our exit from Iraq, or from Kuwait, for that matter. And our Freedom Bird, that big beautiful L-1011 jumbo jet, doesn't fall from the sky over the Atlantic, and fails to crumble into a fiery ball on the tarmac at Pope Air Force Base when we finally touch down on American soil. These are things I have worried will happen. Now, I can start to relax.

A few days after I make it back to Central New York, I call Jessica and arrange to meet her. We begin to see each other seriously.

Everything I experience during those few short months we date seem more special, more precious and sweeter, because I've finally made it "Home". I've been stuck between 2nd and 3rd Base for so long, yearning to reach Home Plate, waiting, expecting to be tagged out. It's impossible to convey just how I feel. Dinners at fine restaurants, strolls along Main Street in Cooperstown, visits to wineries; everything is perfect.

Even now, when I visit Cooperstown and Oneonta, my mind races back to that point.

Curiously, I don't think it would have mattered who I was with at that time; I could have been dating Marge Simpson, and my life

would have been beautiful.
Ugh! Let's not go there...

As often happens, things don't work out with Jessica and me. Looking back, I now realize that I was over-protective of everyone in my life, including her. It was probably very stifling.

Out of my life goes Jessica.

2008: The Year I Was A Serial Dating Victim

I was having no luck with dating. A couple of family friends decided to take matters into their own hands, and attempted to set me up on dates with anything on 2 legs with a pulse. Except guys, of course; even these ladies wouldn't stoop THAT low.

The first candidate was The Whore On The Hill. The local newspaper printed a story about a widow from a rural town who was willing to give $30,000 to any single man who would stay married to her for at least two years. The male victim was required to sign a contract to that effect. The article took up the entire front page and most of the Farm Report. They even included her cell phone number and a photo of this woman, but she was in such deep shadow as to be unrecognizable. Suddenly, the Good Idea Bus ran over Yours Truly, and my name came up as a perfect candidate.

With friends like these, who needs enemies?

First of all, I've held $30K in my hands (Uncle Sugar, Duh!) It's nothing, not enough zeroes, won't even buy a decent SUV.

Question: Where did this widow get the money?

Answer: Probably from the life insurance policy on the last poor bastard who fell for this! This girl could put Bernie Madoff and those email scam artists from Nigeria to shame!

It's a Ponzi scheme of the worst kind...

Second, whoever falls for this doesn't get a dime of the money until after two years of marriage; are you freaking kidding me?

So these two sisters who I've known for years, were trying to tell me that this is an opportunity of a lifetime.

Matchmaker 1: "Think of what you could buy with all that money! Besides, Nana thinks it's a great idea."

Me: "Who the hell is Nana?"

Matchmaker 2: "Our Mom. The kids call her "Nana.""

Me: "Do me a big favor. Tell Nana: No No!"

As I was arguing with the two of them, another "friend" grabbed my cell phone off of the bar, took a photo of one my male friends, and sent it to the Marry Widow's number, complete with the caption: "I think your tractor's sexy!"

The Home Invasion

New Year's, 2008: I'd said goodbye to 2007 in style the night before, and now, nearly 24 hours later, I'm still nursing a hangover. It's snowing heavily, and the wind is howling.
There's a knock at the door. I glance at my watch: 9PM.

Who the hell could it be at this time of night? I'm in NO mood to socialize! I have to work tomorrow.

I open the door a crack. There's a tall woman wearing a white hoodie swaying in front of me. The sweatshirt is covered with red stains; I find myself praying it's not blood.

Me: "Can I help you?"

Woman:" Ish yer name John?"

Her breath lets me know the stains are from spilled red wine, not blood. My prayers are answered, but not for long.

Me: "Yep, I'm John. Can I ask who you might be?"

Woman: "My name's Mary. I'm a friend of Matchmaker 2. Do you have a corkscrew?"

Before I can answer, Bloody Mary pushes on the door and sidesteps me, entering the Sanctuary: my living room. She has a full bottle of red in her hand. She's swaying from side to side, and with my pounding headache, she's literally painful to look at.

Bloody Mary: "Wherez yer bottle opener dammit!"

Me: "I'll go get it!"

Now, I could be a real jerk and tell her to leave right then and there, but I consider myself a gentleman. Plus, my mind is slow to process and I still think of her as a gunshot victim.

So, we're sitting on the couch, but I've made sure there's at least one cushion between us; I don't want to give her any signals that this is going to be anything more than two people sharing a bottle of wine. I'm SO not in the mood.

She informs me that she's a corrections officer. She asks me what I do for a living, and I let her know that my job is testing software. Unfortunately, she finds this fascinating, and begins telling me all about her laptop that is moving so slow and takes so long to get on the Internet. I stifle the nasty urge to tell her that her computer is older than dirt and was probably used at Gettysburg. Instead, I patiently write down some instructions for her to speed it up, by defragging her hard drive and refraining from surfing websites featuring nude male bodybuilders; I'm trying very hard to keep the conversation away from stuff about me. It turns out my efforts are in vain.

Bloody Mary: "We're neighbors! I live three houses down! He he he he!!!"

I hate my life..

The conversation, fortunately, takes a ninety-degree turn.

Bloody Mary: "Didja ever read Jane Austen?"

Me: "Yeah, I recall reading one of her books in-"

Bloody Mary: "I LUFF JANE AUSTEN!!!!!"

Me: "Hey, that's great! Ya know, it's getting late, and I gotta get some-"

Bloody Mary: "You haff kidz?"

Me: "Yes, I have two boys."

Bloody Mary (in a small, pained voice that almost makes me feel sorry for her): "I don't have kids....Never been married, neither."

You keep showing up at strangers' doors drunk as a skunk, and you're going to stay in this drought, I think to myself. I wanna go to bed now! And not with you.

For the next half bottle of wine, she makes small talk. I sit in a defensive posture in the corner of the sofa, and alternately make positive and negative sounds.

Bloody Mary: "I luff kidz! Ya think I would make a good mom?"

Don't do this to yourself, I almost say out loud.

Bloody Mary: "Ya know what I really, REALLY luff?"
Me: "Um, Jane Aust-"

Bloody Mary:" I LUFFFF JANE AUSTEN!!!!!"

Me: "Is that Merlot, by any chance?"

Our girl's eyelids are starting to get heavy, and I'm afraid she's going to pass out on my couch. An unacceptable outcome; mostly because I have a sneaky suspicion that Matchmaker #2 is watching my front porch to see if her friend is going to get lucky and stay the night. Plus I have to go to work in the morning.

Jumpin' crud!

Bloody Mary: "I should go home, don't ya think?"

Me: "That's a good idea!"

Suddenly filled with energy, I spring to my feet and walk to the door, beckoning to her to follow.

Me: "Are you OK to walk home by yourself? "(Again, I'm trying to be a gentleman.)

Bloody Mary: "Oh, no! I'm fine!"

She attempts to show me that she's fine by performing a pirouette in the slush covering the porch. At least, that's what she tries to do, and tumbles into the snow bank next to the steps. I can only make her out by the red splotches on her white sweatshirt. Cars are going by non-stop, and I get a sinking feeling.
I'll bet these people think I shot this woman!

The Arabian Gulf Vacation Club

I decide that we look like a huge zipper.

Me and sixty other soldiers are packed into two rows of what the Air Force calls seats. They're really nothing more than aluminum benches covered in bright red webbing. We're sitting so close together, the troops on either side of me are resting their heads on my shoulders. It's too bad they're both male.

I can't turn my head for fear of waking up the two Sleeping Beauties. But out of the corner of my eye, I can see that all of my fellow passengers are just as uncomfortable as I am. My thighs are positioned adjacent to those of the passenger directly across from me, about three feet away. It's the same awkward arrangement down the length of the C-130 Hercules, hence the Zipper Effect. There are another sixty soldiers on the other side of the plane, enduring their own version of Zipper Hell.

These conditions are scandalous! I thought the Army had the market cornered on being uncomfortable.

Two days before, the stress back at the Crack House had finally gotten to me. Because five of our troops had been peeled off to support the 82nd Airborne down in Dora, the rest of us had had to take on additional duties. We had to, in order to maintain our aggressive schedule of rebuilding the infrastructure around BIAP. We couldn't afford to let up even a bit, because our soldiers had accomplished so much in the past seven months. To slack off now would mean lost momentum. So now, with the Trained Killer and four others detailed out to the 82nd Airborne, I was the Executive Officer, Operations Officer, Public Affairs Officer, Information Security Officer, Automation Officer, Internet Café Manager and Colonel Herriot's driver. I was having serious problems prioritizing, which caused me to have a huge headache. I told myself to suck it up, because our soldiers were doing their jobs AND going outside the wire on missions, daily.

Colonel Herriot, concerned that his Executive Officer was about to have a meltdown, told me that he was sending me on a three-day pass to Qatar.

"Excuse me, Sir? Where the hell is Qatar? I don't want to go on pass, especially to a place with such an ominous name. I can't go, besides; there's too much to do!"

"I'm ordering you to go, Major Ready. My boss did the same thing to me, for my own good. At least, you get to go to Qatar; I only made it to Baghdad. Consider yourself lucky."

The Colonel had just returned from his own three-day pass. He was sent to the Green Zone, to an R&R facility dubbed Freedom Rest. It was a multi-story building with a swimming pool, surrounded by a security fence. On the last day of his pass, he was shaving in the latrine. He heard several loud bangs, and glanced out the window just in time to see three rockets zoom by on their way to the Rashid Hotel, several blocks away. The insurgents had discovered that Paul Wolfowitz, the Deputy Secretary of Defense, was staying there. At least one of the missiles hit their target. Wolfowitz was unscathed, but a lieutenant colonel on another floor was killed.

Freedom Rest was christened Rockets' Rest, and suddenly, everybody was going to Qatar.

The drone of the Hercules' huge propellers has finally lulled me into a nap. Not even the changing pitch of the props awakens me. That only happens when we touch down. Suddenly, a series of sharp jolts release me from my siesta.

Returning to Earth aboard a C-130 can never be classified as a landing; it's more like a controlled crash. A casual observer watching it will see the landing gear make contact with the runway first (if you're lucky to land on a runway). Inside, it's a different story: it seems like everything and everybody hits the ground at the same time. Wheels, passengers, bottles of purified water; we're all in this together. I can only describe it as "bone-jarring". And one bit of truth is bothering me as we descend:

This machine was made by the lowest bidder.

The plane taxi's slowly and the rear cargo ramp begins to drop down. After coming to a stop, we stand up and are directed down the ramp. We're in a hot, dry desolate place. The heat is a shock after the cold and wet of Baghdad.

We file into a Quonset hut and are greeted by smiling Army personnel, which makes me nervous, because people are usually scowling when a large group of soldiers show up somewhere. We sit down, drink the ice-cold water they've given us, and begin to hear about our upcoming three-day reprieve from the war.

The Welcoming Committee give us the standard safety and security briefings all soldiers get when they are new to a duty station, base or foreign country: what not to do, where not to go, what not to say, etc. All of these briefings are written to apprise you of what will happen if you break the rules.

Then comes the final speech, the real reason why we're here: we will be allowed to purchase three alcoholic drinks a day for the next three days!

Now, I have to admit: I'm underwhelmed.

Only three a day? Shit, I've been a Trappist monk for the past eight months! This is a non-starter!

A master sergeant strolls up to me with a huge grin on his face.

What is it with these people?

"Congratulations, Sir! You've just won a sightseeing trip to the capitol of Qatar, Doha!"

"OK, what's the catch, Master Sergeant?"

"Oh, no! There's no catch, Major."

"C'mon, there's ALWAYS a catch."

"Well, Sir, as the senior officer of your group, you've been picked as chaperone for ten soldiers who've signed up to visit the malls in Doha. It'll be fun!"

I knew there was a catch…

"Just be advised that it's the Muslim Holy Month of Ramadan. The US and Qatar have a Status of Forces Agreement between our two nations. If you and any of the soldiers are observed wearing sandals, shorts, tank tops, halter tops, cut-off shirts, drinking alcohol, smoking or chewing tobacco, or chewing gum, you will be charged under Islamic Law."

"Ok. You mean all of the things nineteen and twenty year-old American kids want to do when they get a break from getting shot at?"

"Well, uh, if you want to put it that way, that's correct, Sir."

"You know, I'm gonna pass."

"But, Major, who will chaperone your group?"

"Somebody other than me, Master Sergeant. I was sent here to get away from stress. It's bad enough I'm only allowed three beers a day. I'm not going."

The master sergeant actually looks hurt as I turn away to get on the shuttle bus that will take me to my barracks.

I discover that I'm sharing a room with an Engineer first sergeant who's also stationed at BIAP, and five captains from the 82nd Airborne who've been dodging bullets and rocket propelled grenades in Fallujah. These five are very quiet and keep to themselves. I notice when I introduce myself that their faces are taught, their skin almost like parchment, and their eyes seem to bore straight through me. The oldest is probably thirty, yet they have the demeanor of much older men.

160

Well, if anybody needs a pass, it's these guys. They look like they've seen Hell itself.

Because it's almost drinking time, I shower and change into a polo shirt and jeans, but I'm still wearing my desert combat boots. I feel self-conscious until I notice that everybody else is wearing theirs. Considering where most of us have been, we should be forgiven for our fashion faux pas.

I walk to the drinking pavilion with the first sergeant, who says he's been ordered here by his commander, too. He doesn't feel right drinking while his soldiers are back at the vulnerable side of the airport, playing chicken with rockets and waiting for a night attack on the western perimeter. The wall near his compound reminds him of a similar scene at Mogadishu Airport in Somalia in 1993. And we all know what happened there. I start to worry about my soldiers, too.

I present my military identification card to a soldier at the cash register. The computer will keep track of how many drinks I will buy each day. He swipes my card through a reader, verifies that I'm who I say I am, and gives me three beer tickets. I hand him my cash, and go in search of alcohol. I'm still peeved that I only get to drink three per day.

In this country, I would die in jail.

My fears are for nothing: the beer is from Holland, a brand called Oranjeboom. The bottle proudly labels it as Extra Strong, 12.0 %. After two of them, my "CHECK LIVER" light flashes on.

It's been a long day, and the beer has hit me pretty good, small wonder when I haven't had a drink in about eight months. It's time to go to bed. I stumble to the barracks, and open the door into a scene from the movie, "Fight Club."
The five captains are drunk as lords and wrestling each other on the barracks floor. One of them has a bloody nose from the looks of the large, red smear on the white tiles. They're not as quiet as they were three hours before.

"I love ya, ya little fucker! I love ya! Love ya!"

It turns out these young officers have discovered the base's little secret: there's another club elsewhere on the base. But the computer there isn't connected to its counterpart at the pavilion. So, they just bought three more beers. To top it off, they've found out who the teetotalers are, and bought their tickets, also.

They notice me staring at them, and they stop wrestling very suddenly, like a power switch has been turned off.

"You know, guys, I'm not really that tired. I can come back, later. You go on...doing ...whatever it is... you're doing."

Leaving the barracks, I head over to the payphones, fumble for my calling card and seconds later, hear my young sons' voices. I tell them where I am, but of course, they have no concept. I tell them I love them and we hang up.

The next call is to the Crack House, but I have trouble getting through. This worries me, as it's only 2000; someone should be awake. The concerns of the First Sergeant spoken earlier in the day penetrate my buzz.

Rockets. Not enough security. Ground attack. Mogadishu.

Shit! Something big is going down and I'm here getting hammered a thousand miles away! Isn't that just great!

I decide that I can't sleep until I hear somebody's voice. On the eighth try, I hit paydirt.

Everything is fine, things are going smoothly. See you when you get back. Don't drink too much.
Wow. They don't need me. I can relax.

I fumble in my pocket for my ID card, and run to catch the shuttle to the other club on the base.

The Heartbreak Kid

"Let us cross over the river and rest under the shade of the trees."
-General Thomas " Stonewall" Jackson on his deathbed.

It's late at night. Around 11PM. I call my girlfriend back in New York. I get her answering machine.

As I leave a message, I hear a sound: a gunshot, very close, but muffled.

Somebody had a negligent discharge. Didn't clear their weapon.

A negligent discharge occurs when a soldier fails to ensure that all of the ammunition has been fired or removed from their weapon. The standard clearing procedure-at least in the Army-involves posting personnel at an entrance or gate to a base; that individual has to check every weapon as it comes through. The soldier removes the magazine, and pulls back and locks the bolt on the weapon. The guard runs a metal rod all the way down the barrel; if there is a bullet in there, the rod will hit it.

After ensuring that there are no bullets in the weapon, the soldier will let the bolt ride forward, place the muzzle in a sand-filled drum, and pull the trigger. If everyone's done his job, there should not be a round fired. The sand in the clearing barrel is there just in case.

So, in my mind, after I hear that solitary gunshot, it's obvious that someone hasn't followed procedure.

Somebody's ass is going to be in a sling. A negligent discharge is punishable by a letter of reprimand, at least.

You sorry bastard!

It couldn't possibly be an attack. We're so far deep inside the base. The main entrance to the airport is at least three quarters of a mile away. If the Bad Guys attack, they wouldn't just send in one guy with an AK-47. Somebody screwed up, that's all.

I sit down to wait for my girlfriend to call me back.

Within a few seconds, I hear somebody yelling. It's a man. His voice is loud, pleading. It rises in panic, going up several octaves as he shouts repeatedly.

"Somebody please help me!"

I run toward the stairs. At the bottom, I see 2 women who are frantic. I remember the terror in their wide eyes. Their faces are white, drained of color. They are running into the foyer, a flurry of motion. They're yelling that they need a doctor. The Division Surgeon lives in our building. Our own PA is in the Officers' Quarters. I yell as loud as I can for him as I run upstairs to find Division Surgeon for the First Armored. I hear the PA answer.

"Be right there!"

I climb the stairs to find the doctor.

What the hell floor is he on?

My brain's scrambling to remember. I run up to each floor of the Crack House, 2 steps at a time. My heart is pounding, and I feel like I'm starting to panic. I don't even know what happened.

I can't find him! Shit!

I run downstairs. I hear a commotion out in front of the building. I run toward it. Don't see the PA, anywhere. He was in bed the last I checked. God, I hope he gets out here. There's an emergency of some sort, I don't know what.

I don't want to let anybody down.

I see the female soldiers standing over something in the parking lot. There are 2 or 3 more people there. I don't recognize them.

They are looking at someone lying there. On his back. Head tilted back, eyes closed, arms splayed out. He's wearing Desert Camo. I'm starting to think that maybe he is passed out; unconscious. I can see his rank. He's an officer.

Then, I see the M16 off to one side. The concrete near it is wet, shiny.

I glance back at his head. His teeth seem to be missing. I see a massive wound in the back of his head.

Oh God, no! No!

I get closer. I'm still about 30 feet away. I'm thinking: "This guy's had it". There's nothing anybody can do. I just know it. The officer, who only short minutes before had been a living, breathing person, is now only a husk, devoid of life.

The Division Surgeon and our PA sprint past me and start working on the victim. He looks like a mannequin, pasty faced. White, not just pale. Our CO, COL Herriott, joins them. I see him stepping over pieces of bone and what looks like brain.

I can't look away. I want to tear my eyes away, but I can't.

People start showing up from all over. The MPs arrive and begin setting up a perimeter around the scene. A SGT walks up to me and asks me if I'm a witness. I tell him I heard a shot and remember exactly what time it was. It's time-stamped on my phone.

He tells me that he needs me to fill out a statement. The MP asks me to wait off to one side. I stand there for 2 hours waiting to be interviewed. Mercifully, someone has thrown a plastic poncho over the body. Suddenly, an MP lieutenant shows up and sees the covered figure. He yells at everybody for disturbing the crime scene. He makes the SGT take the poncho off.

I don't think I'll be able to stare at this spot on the wall very much longer, but I don't want to look at the body.

Please, God!

After a sleepless, restless night, I reluctantly go outside and walk toward the scene. It's no longer cordoned off. All the blood and bone has been removed, and there is nothing to indicate that a candle had been snuffed out barely 7 hours before. The parking lot is back to its busy, frenetic pace. HUMVEEs and trucks are driving over the spot where there had been so much anguish and despair last night.

It's like nothing happened.

Two weeks later, I'm surfing the Internet. I come across a website published by the Washington Post: Faces of the Fallen. It lists every casualty of the War on Terror, regardless of the cause of death. Like a moth to a flame, I search for the last name of the soldier whose life ended in front of the Crack House.

There he is; smiling, proud, and confident, in his graduation photo. No cares, no worries. On top of the world.

What went wrong, buddy? What was it that ate away at you inside, that made you think this was the only option? Didn't you realize the young kids getting killed all around you would have given anything to be keep living? Why did you throw it away?

We're all human: everyone in his or her life gets despondent or overwhelmed at some point and considers suicide. There, I said it.

We think about doing it, but something pulls us back from the brink, a friend, some kind words, a realization that things will get better. This too shall pass....

It doesn't have to be this way. No matter how bad things get, no matter how insurmountable the obstacle, we can always reinvent ourselves, move, change jobs or relationships, start anew.

His family was devastated, obviously. Unanswered questions. An empty chair during the holidays and birthdays. The promise of grandchildren. All these hopes cut short on a cold night half a world away.

And of course, the broken heart of a father, who heard your last cry of anguish.

166

Hell Week

Thanksgiving Week, November 2003.

Other than early July, when 2 of our soldiers were wounded in action, this was one of the most traumatic weeks of our deployment. On the 22nd, the DHL cargo plane was hit by a Surface to Air Missile (SAM). On Sunday, Colonel Herriot's father died. The next day, as I was consoling him, I received a Red Cross Message informing me that my uncle had passed away. And of course, someone always has to ask the question: "What else could go wrong?"

The building next door caught fire. That's what could go wrong.

The conflagration begins as an electrical fire in one of the airport's maintenance hangars, which just so happens to be situated ten feet from the Crack House. I'm looking out the window at the alley between the 2 buildings and I spot flames licking around one of the office doorways. Soon, I watch soldiers running into the building trying to retrieve the personnel records for the First Armored Division Headquarters. These records included fingerprint cards and panographic x-rays, items which are routinely used for identification. This is presumably why these young soldiers are risking being horribly burned by running straight into an inferno.

I call DIVARTY on the Force Protection Net. They're not impressed by the report of a fire.

Operator: Oh, the airport fire department is running a training exercise. It's just a simulation.

Me: That's one hell of a realistic simulation! I can see flames coming out of the doorway, and I don't see any firemen.

Operator: Click!

Sunovabitch!! The asshole hung up on me!

By now, the flames are shooting out from under the sheet metal roof, and there is a distinct shortage of firefighting personnel in the area. I will never forget the bizarre sight of young troops running out of the hangar burdened with file drawers, while flames are licking around the doorframe.

Fuck this! I call the Fire Department on the radio.

When I get hold of the operator from DIVARTY, I'm gonna shove the handset down his throat…

It is now blatantly obvious that we need to evacuate the Crack House. Our team begins to grab all of our sensitive items such as weapons, night vision goggles, radio encryption gear, etc. We'll just have to take our chances with our personal belongings.

Personal belongings! Oh, shit! The 12 Oriental rugs I bought are in my hooch! I was going to mail them tomorrow. The rugs are rolled up and wrapped in plastic, ready to go. That's what I get for procrastinating! It seemed like such a monumental task to load up the rugs into the HUMVEE, run it over to the Army Post Office, and wait in line for over an hour. Damn!

So, we're evacuating the Crack House and we notice the Airport Fire Department show up with their tanker. They're standing there watching the fire. Very innocently, I ask them when they plan on extinguishing the fire. The fire chief's response: "We don't put out fires; we keep them from spreading to other buildings."

OK

Suddenly, a long rumble and vibration comes from underground. It feels like an earthquake. What the hell?

OK, we've got war, we've got fire, and now an earthquake! What's next, a cholera epidemic?

I though this shit only happened in the Bible….

The rumbling is not an earthquake; deep in the basement, the

Iraqis had stockpiled artillery shells before the war. The flames have finally reached the shells and they're exploding underground. As it turns out, alongside the explosives, are stored thousands of rounds of AK-47 ammunition. They reach critical mass and enter the confined space of the courtyard between the buildings. Tracer rounds crack overhead and ricochet off the walls.

I'm going to die here, and the enemy doesn't have to lift a finger. My demise will be a death by proxy.

You can't make this shit up...

Crouching down, I sprint down the alley, looking for Sponge Bob and the Tooth Faeries, who are quartered in the courtyard, directly opposite the burning building. I see Sponge Bob struggle out of the entrance to his hooch, a cardboard box on each shoulder. I catch a glimpse inside: Oriental rugs.

"Sir, we need to get out of here now! Run to me!"

"I gotta save the rugs!"

"Screw the rugs! Is there anybody else in there?"

"No, everybody's out!"

Out of the corner of my eye, I see Mini Me, the short dentist, running out of the smoke, bullets tracing fiery paths above him, a box perched precariously on his shoulder. There's a good chance a rug is inside.

"I thought you said everybody was out!"

"Except for him, everybody's out!"

I hate this movie...

The Night the Boom Booms Got Too Close

"I have a catapult. Give me all the money, or I will fling an enormous rock at your head!"

- Early Roman bank robbery note

From the third month of our time at Baghdad International Airport, the base was mortared and rocketed at least once a week. The shells never made it over to our side of the airport. They usually impacted on the West side, on the other side of the runway, and always at night.

After we heard the explosions, we would scramble out of our building and look to the West, to spot the inevitable flames, black clouds and the flashing red lights of the emergency vehicles. Even though we were in a combat zone, even though we were on the same base, I always thought of their predicament as Somebody Else's War. And I would always say to myself:

"I'm glad I don't live over there."

Checkpoint One, the main entrance to the airport, was attacked at night several times in the Fall of 2003. It had to be one of the most heavily guarded gates in all of Iraq, and one of the most important, because it was the entrance to a major transportation hub, and therefore a key to rebuilding Iraq. That's why the Coalition Forces didn't screw around when it was time to defend it. They called in the AC-130 Spooky gunship, an unholy alliance between one of those Hercules transports and one badass Gatling gun. That gun fires 3000 rounds per minute and is guided by radar. When it speaks, it spits out a seemingly unbroken stream of fire. To give some perspective, every fifth bullet coming down is a tracer, or incendiary marking round. Needless to say, if you get hit by one of those guns, you're no longer much good to anybody.

They say your immune system breaks down.

I'm glad I'm not an insurgent.

For some stupid ass reason, every time Spooky arrived to crash the party, some of us would climb the 8 stories of our building-The Crack House -and watch the show from the roof. We would almost always comment that that was not really a smart thing to do. And almost always, we would do the same thing the next time Spooky arrived to clean up.

"You know, this might have been a bad idea..."

The enemy waited until nightfall to attack; the Explosive Ordnance Disposal personnel used the daylight hours to rattle our nerves. Both the Army and Air Force bomb squads would hold controlled detonations just about every hour. We were able to distinguish between both groups' handiwork because the Army would give a warning over the radio. The Air Force, because they thought they were better than the Army and chafed at their regulations and procedures, blew off this practice and sent chunks of Iraqi real estate skyward at frequent and irregular intervals.

And then, finally, the rockets made it over to our patch.

I had just come back from leave for 2 weeks in the States. When I arrived on my flight from Kuwait, bringing me back to reality, one of the sergeants in my battalion arrived to take me back to the Crack House. I casually asked him how things had been since I was gone. He began to hem and haw and tried to avoid the question.

"Well..."
"What do you mean by 'Well'?"
"Well, we've been getting hit by rockets on our side for about the last 3 nights."
"Hey. That's greaaaaat..."

The bad guys left me alone that night. I started to feel like I had brought some good luck with me from home. But the next evening, the luck ran out.

I'm downstairs on the first floor, in our Internet cafe, christened the Naugahyde Ballroom in honor of the vinyl chairs and couches in there. Just 10 personal computers in a perpetually dusty room with an entertainment center at one end. It's all connected to civilization via satellite: our little pocket of Normal.

It's about 2130, which is usually when I go for my nighttime run. It's the only time I'm able to break away, since there are too many bullshit meetings during daylight hours. Plus, I find that it helps me sleep better. Three laps around the big parking lot out front equals one mile. Tonight, for some reason, I decide against it. The thought of not exercising makes me feel guilty, but I'm unable to leave my chair.

A half dozen of our troops are in the café. I'm checking my e-mail, when the keyboard suddenly rises up and hits my chin. The room is shaking and a noise so loud that it seems to be part of me resonates through the building. Dust and bits of plaster streams drop from the ceiling. The windows above our heads, only days before taped up to reduce the spraying of shattered glass, cave inwards and send shards sliding down the walls and flying toward us.

More duct tape? Yep, more duct tape.

My heart's pounding. I can't breathe, choking on fine dust. My body's shaking like a blender and my legs feel like they're rooted in the floor. Somehow, I remember I'm getting paid to be in charge, and I break into a run, beginning to shout for everybody to hit the floor. But, before I can yell anything coherent, I trip over a power cable and perform a Triple Salchow over the back of one of the couches, landing face up. Just about knocks the wind out of me.

My first thoughts: Four short days ago, I was making a snow-man with my two young boys, and now I'm trying to pull my buttons off to get closer to the floor.

Whatever they're lobbing at us, the next one's going right up my left nostril.

"Why did I come back here?"

Another blast rocks the building. And then, silence.

I can hear people yelling close by, and I run outside. Remembering there was an MCI phone trailer in the parking lot outside our courtyard, I pray that none of the two dozen or so troops waiting in line are hit.

I strain to see into the darkness. At first glance, all I see is smoke drifting along the pavement. There's an eerie silence; it fills me with a terrible foreboding of what I might see out there. The smoke gradually dissipates, along with the silence. And then, there they are: a crowd of scared kids stream into our lot. None of them seems to be wounded; at least I see no blood. In the background I can see three soldiers who got back in line for the phones, not willing to let the enemy rockets keep them from calling home.

The "all clear" hasn't been sounded yet. No one is allowed to be out in the open, so the soldiers take refuge in our building. We let the troops use our TOC telephone to call their units and let them know they are OK. I strike up a conversation with a troop who looks like he just graduated high school. I ask how long he's been in Iraq. The young soldier tenses up; it's suddenly obvious I've committed a terrible sin by asking.

He turns toward me, and answers through gritted teeth: "Since about 0800 this morning, Sir."

>INSERT NERVOUS LAUGHTER HERE<

As it turns out, there are three rockets that have hit, two of them near the MCI phone trailer. By divine intervention, the troops waiting in line have been shielded by some equipment. The shrapnel from the blasts have transformed a couple of huge generators into avant-garde metal sculptures. I count at least 100 holes in one of them.

At first light, I walk the parking lot to the rocket impact points. The Crater Analysis Team is busy inspecting the craters in the tarmac. These guys determine the direction from which rockets, artillery shells, and mortar rounds originate, the better to pinpoint the enemy's location. It's more of an art than a science, but it's pretty accurate.

This morning, after consulting their chicken bones and tealeaves, they determine that the missiles passed within 200 yards of our building: Miracle Number Two.

As I stand watching, I suddenly realize that if I'd been running like I did every other night, at any point as I ran my laps I'd have been sprayed with hot metal fragments. A shiver runs down my spine.

There, but for the grace of God...

When Life Gives You Liberty, Make IEDs

In February 2004, my CA battalion is attending the Grand Re-Opening of the al-Makessib School, located outside the airport perimeter. They are joined by the unit that is replacing us, a CA team from California, and some Air Force photojournalists.

The rebuilding of this school has been our top priority since the attempted shoot down of the Airbus four months ago. 1AD has made it clear: no matter what, we need to get that village on our side so that the enemy cannot target aircraft from right outside the FOB; Classic "Hearts and Minds". I'm not able to go because I have to brief the Assistant Division Commander of the 1st Armored Division. Lucky me.

Now, our CA team has been coordinating the re-building of this school since November, spent $300,000 of confiscated funds on it, so we're very proud of our efforts. A crew from an American news agency has asked permission to cover the story, and I'm "voluntold" to be the Public Affairs rep for this ceremony. This is our last project before we head south to Kuwait on our way home.

During the briefing, I feel, rather hear, an explosion in the distance. I shrug it off; the EOD teams are constantly disposing of munitions at remote areas on the FOB. "Just another day in Paradise", I mentally joke to myself.

I trudge back to the Crack House after the brief. Just as I reach the building entrance, my cell phone rings. It's the reporter, Jim Davis.

"Are your guys OK?" he asks.

"Well, I don't know. I just got back from a meeting. And why wouldn't they be OK? What happened out there?" Panic begins to rise inside me.

"After the ceremony, an IED went off right next to your team's vehicles. We left there by a different route."

177

My jaw drops. That old, familiar feeling begins to wash over me. I gather my wits and try to get more information. "This is the first I've heard about this! Did you see anybody go down?"

"No. But it was a pretty big explosion. I'm afraid they may have been hit."

"I'll have to get back to you."

This can't be happening! Not again! And, not on the eve of our departure!

I frantically make phone calls to the Division Force Protection guys, and to anybody who can tell me what's happened. Force Protection tells me everyone is fine and they are being debriefed. Deafened and shook up, of course.

While I was on the phone, I notice the Trained Killer cleaning his M16 on the window ledge, mumbling to himself as he's staring down two Iraqis working on the big generator in the courtyard below. I get a sick feeling he's about to go off and do one of those Texas Tower numbers. I asked him if he was OK, and I told him to settle down and that I was just as upset as he was.

I hear Jim Davis' voice, again, but it's not on my cell. I'm flabbergasted as to where his voice is coming from. Then, I realize it's coming from our break room. Like out of a scene in The Twilight Zone, I walk slowly through the doorway toward his voice. It's coming from the satellite TV. He's contacted the first available live show broadcasting back in the States, Imus In The Morning. There's Don Imus intently listening to Davis' live report. He has just been with a CA unit at a school opening, and an IED has gone off while they were finishing taping. He also tells the entire world that the unit's Public Affairs rep, Major Ready, has no idea what has just happened to his own unit!

Here we go, again, this is so wild! I say it here, and it comes out there....

Jim Davis is a former Army Reserve Captain, a chopper pilot, and I've figured because of this, he's above punking out another military guy. Turns out I was wrong.

Because of this one incident, I trust reporters about as far as I can spit canal water. I have made the mistake of not realizing that Teague was a reporter first, and ex-military, second.

It gets worse.

Our team returns to our building. The looks on their faces as they walk in are unforgettable. They look so defeated and used up. I don't understand how they can walk, as their eyes are wide, unfocused, seemingly unseeing.

I've finally witnessed the Thousand Yard Stare.

Everybody who was at the event has been deafened. The troops are practically yelling when they tell me what happened. Colonel Herriot is the only individual who has a wound: a half moon-shaped laceration on his calf. His HUMVEE has a couple of large holes in the back, right next to the gas tank. Thankfully, the IED had been planted in a pile of construction debris: lathe, drywall, etc. So, the physical wounds could be worse.

The slap in the face from the people in the village is what hurts even more. All that work, the coordination, the dozens of trips outside the wire into harm's way, the gesture of kindness to a village, all for the purpose of allowing young children to once again be able to learn, wiped out.

They tell me that the villagers were celebrating and cheering after the explosion. They apparently find more satisfaction in watching the "Occupiers" get bloodied than having a functioning school, once again. The Commander of the BIAP Quick Reaction Force asks Colonel Herriot whether he wants to go back into the village to find the perpetrators.

The colonel replies that he doesn't care if the entire fucking village-including the rebuilt elementary school-is razed.

A nice guy can only be pushed so far, after all.

We watch Jim Davis report the incident on the evening news later on. Hardly any mention of all the good our soldiers had done over the past year. It's just the same old story of an Army unit getting hit.

On a whim, Sergeant McDonald decides to "Google" our unit name, 414th CA Battalion. The third link down is a page from the Coalition Provisional Authority website, showing our itinerary for the next 3 weeks: times, dates, names, cell numbers and grid locations. Everything an insurgent could ever want to plan an ambush.

Someone from our brigade has given all this to the OCPA webmaster, and they put it out on there on the Web for everyone to see, including Al Qaeda!

Nice job, dickheads!

By now, I'm livid, frothing at the mouth. I want someone to pay for this. If we can't find the guys who pushed the detonator, then my next target is the ass clown who probably gave them the opportunity. I call down to Brigade in the Green Zone.

"I want to know who posted all of that sensitive information on the OCPA website. He or she just about got my soldiers greased!"

"Oh, we have no idea how that info got up on that site."

"Well, damnit! I work in the information technology field. So I know somebody had to edit the website. The shit doesn't just grow on there!"

"Well, it's your battalion's itinerary; maybe you posted it on the web."

I slam the phone down, totally pissed. Later on that night, I relate the day's events to an officer on the Division staff. I can tell he is also full of righteous indignation. Instead of fuming silently like myself, he smiles and asks for my Brigade's phone number.

"I'm gonna fix their little red wagon!" he says.

He gets the same colonel I've spoken with earlier.

"How y'all doin'" he drawls pleasantly. "Now, I understand y'all been givin' the 414th a real hard time about the incident where they almost got blown up today. Yer sayin' it may be their fault. Well I'll tell ya, I didn't have a lot of friends at the University of Texas, but one I did works on the staff of General Schoomaker, ya know, the Chief of Staff of the whole, damn Army?"

He suddenly drops the folksy voice. "And if you think that your idea of conducting an investigation is 'blaming the victim', it'll be my mission in life to make sure you wish you NEVER put on the uniform. If you keep going down this trail, I'll have so many people breathing down your neck! Knock this shit off, right NOW!

Don't mess with Texas!

We never hear another peep out of Brigade.

The Death of a Thousand Cuts

0700 hours. DIVARTY Headquarters.

The Intelligence Officer, or S2, conducts his daily briefing, talking about the latest insurgent capabilities and developments. It always seems to be the same thing, day after day. This morning, he tells us something new: information comes from reliable sources that the insurgents will be using ambulances as VBIEDS (Vehicle Borne Improvised Explosive Devices). In layman's terms, truck bombs.

Six months ago, just after Saddam's regime had been toppled, massive looting occurred all over Baghdad. The Iraqi police had been disbanded. Crowds of people, knowing there was no one to stop them, stole everything that wasn't nailed down. Ambulances used by the Iraqi Red Crescent, an organization similar to the Red Cross, had disappeared.

Now it appears they're about to come out of hiding, with deadly consequences. This bit of information sticks in my brain. It's still there an hour later, as myself, LTC Winston, and Abbas reenter BIAP Checkpoint One after meeting our contractors. Our HUMVEE winds its way through the slalom of barricades, the Iraqi contractors following us in their civilian vehicles.

Then, it's there, right in front of us: a solitary vehicle moving slowly toward the overpass that separates the road from Division Main. The driver seems confused: he moves forward a bit, hesitates, reverses, and stops. An ambulance, clearly marked with a red crescent.

This is it! This is what the S2 talked about, not even an hour ago! They're going to blow up the division headquarters!

I can make out the two bearded men in the cab.

How did a truck with explosives make it past the checkpoint? Who searched the son of a bitch? Did anybody?

My brain goes on autopilot as I gun the HUMVEE around the ambulance and swerve in front of it, blocking its forward movement. I can't let it through the overpass. Once it gets past that, there's no stopping it. Division Main is the nerve center for the entire Baghdad security mission. There are hundreds of unsuspecting soldiers working there.

I jump out of the drivers' seat, and move quickly toward the ambulance, my M-16 aimed at the driver. LTC Winston has his 9mm out, pointed at the same target. Abbas is yelling loudly at the two men in Arabic.

"Get your hands up on the windshield, or you're dead men!"

My heart is doing laps around my chest, and I'm holding my breath as I try to keep my hands and the rifle steady. Time has slowed to a crawl, and a million thoughts race through my mind:

I can't let 'em get through to Division Main!

These two guys are about to sacrifice themselves along with Winston, myself and our translator, right here, right now.

This is my own personal 9/11.

Awful sorry about this Pat and Mike. Daddy loves you!

I can see the driver's face in my rifle sights. His eyes and mouth are wide open, a mask of fear. The front sight post of my M-16 bisects his forehead. All that needs to happen is for me to gently squeeze the trigger, just the slightest pressure, just like they taught me at Fort Knox over 23 years ago.

The driver is immobile, there's no angry look on his face; he's not yelling or mouthing the words "Allahu Akbar" (God is great), or anything that indicates he's about to perform the ultimate sacrifice. Matter of fact, he looks as surprised and shocked as I feel.

Maybe I'm wrong. Maybe I'm within a hair's breath of snuffing out an innocent life. I wish somebody or something would give me a sign, either way.

My sign comes: The driver's left hand leaves the windshield. It drops to his side, near the door.
Whatthefuckishedoing?! Is he gonna hit the detonator? Oh, shit!

I'm still clueless about his intentions. I know Winston and Abbas are close by, but they're out of my peripheral vision. My whole world is confined to the thirty feet between my eyes and those of the bearded man behind the glass. And I still can't bring myself to pull the trigger.

The driver's door pops open, and he jumps out, kneeling on the macadam in front of me. He's shaking like a leaf, and I notice that he's soiled himself out of fear. The other man gets out and prostrates himself on the roadway. Another group of soldiers happening by searches the ambulance, while Abbas questions the two men.

As it turns out, they are an ambulance crew on their first trip to Airport Village, the small settlement of airport employees located next to BIAP. They simply got lost: a nearly tragic case of mistaken identity.

This is a drama that's been played out and repeated probably hundreds of times in Iraq and Afghanistan. Soldiers have to make life and death decisions with what information they have. They're trained, from Day One, to neutralize a threat. Now, they have to be prepared to do the same, but exhibit restraint.

If a soldier hesitates, it could mean death for his buddies and himself. If he acts on what little information he has, he can take an innocent life, creating an international incident. It's the same dilemma for law enforcement. And, unless you've faced it, you cannot say what you'd do in that situation.

It still bothers me that I couldn't pull the trigger.

It's just after the school bombing in Al-Makessib. Sitting at my desk, I feel a numbness that permeates my entire body and soul. At this point, I am no longer afraid. I'm jaded, disheartened, disgusted, totally pissed, but no longer afraid of death. Because of all the shit that's happened over the past ten months, the friends lost to the insurgency, our own soldiers being wounded, the stupidity and incompetence of our leaders-and my own, the realization hits me that I'm not leaving Iraq alive.

If we were in a courtroom, and all of the bad things that have occurred were presented as evidence, the verdict would come back: Doomed! It's that simple; my luck will not hold out. The only way to attend to my responsibilities is to make peace with death. Once the fear is gone, I can do my job. And if I do that, and the others do theirs, maybe I'll see my boys again.

The rest of my life will be gravy.

The Potty Patrol

When you're in the Middle East, there are several warnings you should really, really heed. One of the most important is: "Don't drink the water!" This is obviously because of the probable existence of parasites in it, like those amoebas you studied in Biology class that are alive, but you don't know why. Drinking unpurified water in Iraq almost always leads to the condition known as "Saddam's Revenge". Forget work; forget any activity unless it involves sitting in pain for hours. There is also a good chance of severe nausea, in which case you'll throw up stuff you ate as a child.

Because of the loss of fluids from diarrhea and vomiting, your body will become severely dehydrated. And you will have IV bags hooked up to you for the next two days, replacing the electrolytes you've squandered.

The local food was an even worse source of illness.

One of the duties of Civil Affairs soldiers is: "Thou shall sit down with the locals and eat their food, and you will see that it is good, and be grateful". CA troops are in the business of working with the locals, and frequently are invited to the homes of tribal leaders, sheiks, etc. As I mentioned previously, it's considered very bad manners to refuse an invite from Arabs to eat their food at one of these meetings. On a side note, I know a number of CA operators who served in Bosnia in the 90's, and they were actually allowed to accept alcoholic drinks from Serbs in the performance of their duties. I recalled those stories with envy while I was in Iraq; I figured it was just my luck to be deployed to a region where alcohol was outlawed. "Well, I figured, it's the only war we've got, so make the best of it."

I had the misfortune of being invited to dinner at a sheik's home, where we were served huge quantities of food that I couldn't identify, with the exception of my new best friend: rice. Good old rice! No matter what the Iraqi's threw in it-spices, raisins, vegetables, an entire broiled fish-I think it was staring at me-I could count on it tasting good, and not have to worry too much about getting sick. That was not the case with the lamb.

I've never liked eating lamb in the first place; growing up, lamb was foreign. My mom never served it at home (she was too busy cooking up the venison Dad brought back from one of his many hunting trips), and it was not available at fast food joints. This was OK by me, because I've never enjoyed eating food that leaves a chum line on the plate.

So here's the sheik serving me up lamb, using his bare hands to tear the meat from the bone and dumping it on my plate. Both bare hands, if you get my drift; we're in the Middle East. I'll allow you to conjure up that image by yourself, and not fault you for throwing up in your mouth.

I force myself to chew some of the lamb, and will it down my throat. Convulsing, my head swivels to the right, and I spot Big D. Big D loves lamb, cannot get enough of lamb. And right now, he's eating lamb like it's his job. I get his attention, and making sure no one's looking, I expertly flip my lamb portions onto his plate, like it was meant to be. And I ask for more rice.

The next day, I'm at a Civil Affairs planning session at Division HQ. Each Civil Affairs unit in the Baghdad Area of Operations is required to brief the Commanding General on their responsibilities. It falls on me, the Battalion XO, to brief the general on ours.

During a short break, the ire of Saddam Hussein makes its presence known deep inside me. I tense up, and I begin to sweat profusely. It's all I can do to hold myself together, for the sake of all living things, but especially for everyone in the room.

Oh, no!
This is bad! See also: not good.

I can't afford to relax at all. I stand up slowly. Everyone begins staring at me, probably because waves of perspiration are running down my face, and I'm sure my lips have disappeared from concentrating so hard. Backing away from the table, I head for the door. I'm shuffling along a dark tunnel.

Captain Johnny Cougar, who's helping me brief, calls out to me. He sounds a mile away.

"Sir, you can't leave!"
"You lying motherfucker!" I think to myself.

I'm in the hallway, heading to the door that leads to the outside latrine area: a row of beautiful-in my current frame of mind-portable toilets. It's Division Headquarters, where the generals and other high-ranking brass live: they have the extended cab Port-a-Potties here. Reams of toilet paper and boxes of sanitary wipes. Paradise! Hell, they probably have a manservant in each one of those things.

Just before the exit I spot two figures in desert camouflage. Oh shit, it's the Division Commander and another general, deep in conversation!

"Why here? Why now?"

The generals are blocking my escape route, and in order to go around them, I have to acknowledge their presence and greet them, very respectively. They might even ask me questions, like where the hell do I think I'm going. But answering will expend valuable energy needed for more important...muscles.

At this point, I decide that a Royal Flush beats 3 Stars, so I shuffle around them. To my credit, I stop, turn my head, make eye contact and move on. It'll have to do. I keep my eyes on the prize and head for the nearest portable toilet.

"There's no toilet paper! Nothing, not a scrap!"

Somewhere, from within the deepest recesses of my brain, a piece of information floats to the surface, and reminds me that there are latrines in front of the Crack House, about two hundred yards away.

Might as well be in the next solar system…

Exhausted, I maneuver crab-like toward The Promised Land. In the nearest latrine, I find the rewards of my suffering: toilet paper! The Port-a-Potty is tiny, blistering hot and smells absolutely terrible, but seems like the Kingdom of Heaven right now. Muttering prayers of thanks, I get down to business.

VROOOMMM!!!!! The whirring of an engine brings me back to reality. It's the SST!
"No! Not the Shit-Sucking Truck! Not now!"

The waste removal contract was awarded to a Kuwaiti firm, and they have arrived to do their job, just when I thought I was in the clear.

The doors are being slammed open in the latrines around me. Even though the door to mine is bolted, I grab the doorframe in defiance.

"Mistah, Mistah! Clean, clean!"
"No! Bad time! Go away!"
"Mistah! Make Quick!"

I'm desperate now, so I run the barrel of my M-16 through the latch; it'll take a hammer to dislodge it.
"Go away!"

I realize now that my life has become a complete sham: I'm a victim in a Port-a-Potty hostage crisis.

Damn lamb!

The Highway to Hell Runs in Both Directions

The Baghdad Airport Road. ROUTE IRISH. Ambush Alley. Whatever name you associate with it, the mere thought of driving that 8-mile strip of asphalt was enough to give you chills in 140-degree heat.

Nothing good happened on that road.

It was more than just an access road for Baghdad International Airport, or the connection between that major transportation hub and the Green Zone. It eventually became a symbol for the deteriorating security situation in Iraq. Immediately after the invasion in early 2003, traveling back and forth between BIAP and the Green Zone was as normal as driving to work back in the States. The road was christened "ROUTE IRISH" after Notre Dame University. Sure, you had to have security-whether it be gun trucks, or extra vehicles with long guns-but going back and forth to the palace complex was routine. Around the May-June time frame, things started to go to shit.

The insurgents-former Baathist Party hacks, disgruntled Sunni and Shiite Iraqi's, imported Al Qaeda fighters, or whomever-soon saw the road as a perfect place to hold a turkey shoot. Snipers were positioned along its length, ready to fire from beneath overpasses and behind date palms. Then, the Bad Guys emplaced IEDs, or Improvised Explosive Devices, which is just a fancy name for Booby Traps.

These were low-tech bombs consisting of munitions that had been stockpiled by Saddam and cached all over Iraq. Artillery shells, mortar rounds, and even high explosives from anti-tank mines were used. By some estimates, there were close to one million tons of high explosives hidden all over the country, just for the taking. And they were.

A roadside bomb could be in a hole dug in a median strip, hidden in a length of fake concrete curbing, or even in an animal carcass. A safe bet was that there was an IED inside an empty cardboard box, sitting innocently beside the road. The main problem was determining which one. What do young Americans do in a country where littering was lawful and even encouraged? They tossed the cardboard boxes in which they received their bottled water right out their HUMVEE windows. These white boxes with blue Arabic lettering were sprinkled like toadstools along ROUTE IRISH.

The first generation of IEDS along the Airport Road were command-detonated by wire strung from the bomb back to the Bad Guy holding the detonator. After detonation, the insurgent had to high tail it out of the area rather quickly to avoid apprehension. Then came the radio-controlled family of roadside bombs, and they allowed the enemy to trigger the bombs from a greater distance. These were detonated via cell phones, pagers, portable phones and car alarms. The U.S. military devised methods to jam the radio frequencies that operated on these devices.

Eventually, the enemy and our military engaged in the ultimate game of one-upmanship: constantly creating and retooling methods of defeating each other. Of course, the insurgents had an advantage: they controlled a nearly limitless supply of high explosives from which to create their bombs. But the loss of even one of our servicemen or women was a defeat. In one particularly horrific incident, an M1A2 Abrams tank had run over an IED made up of fifteen 152mm artillery shells. The detonation had sent the turret flying. No amount of armor can withstand that. By 2007, over 60% of all American KIAs were due to IEDs.

Ambush Alley was where your senses were always on edge, eyes constantly scanning while your vehicle made its way through eight miles of No Man's Land. Your heart started beating faster and your throat got drier as soon as you left BIAP's Checkpoint One: Main Gate. Your vehicle swerved around concrete or sand-filled barricades, and traversed shallow trenches cut in the asphalt, methods employed to slow down would-be truck bombers. (these barriers were at both the in and out lanes; the insurgents didn't obey Wrong Way signs). Then, you saw the statue.

The Flying Man was a monument in the median strip between

he highway lanes. It commemorated an ancient astronomer who attempted to fly and died trying. A dark, foreboding statue with huge wings, it was the unofficial demarcation point from the airport and safety. Beyond it was The Unknown.

Then, as if by instinct, we would drive like mad down the three-lane roadway. You wouldn't slow down, and you sure as hell wouldn't stop, for anything. If there were civilian vehicles in the way, we swerved around them. To be courteous was to invite death; to live was to drive like we owned the place.

Approaching an overpass, we would go under it in one lane and emerge in another, to confuse any snipers or bombers who were waiting in ambush, or anyone acting as lookouts. The only defense was constant change. To be predictable was a recipe for disaster.

Every so often, you could tag along with another convoy, the bigger the better. One day, I accompanied Colonel Herriot on a trip to the Green Zone. The convoy we merged with was a long line of fuel tanker trucks, vehicles you really didn't want to be near if they were attacked. This was the only large convoy that was heading out, though, and the two pairs of AH-64 Apache gunships flying cover for it made us feel invincible.

Somebody go ahead and fuck with us. Try it!

As we neared the palace complex, however, we watched as the long line of tankers exited the Airport Road, heading elsewhere in Baghdad. With them went the attack helicopters and our bravado. We were still at least a mile from the palace complex, with only two HUMVEES, and no extra security. I suddenly felt like one of those gray beetles you see when you pull a log off the ground. It was like every insurgent in Baghdad had cross hairs on us. When we finally entered the Green Zone, I was shaking in my boots.

It's January 2004. We're headed to the Green Zone, all of us. Our brigade has a new commander, and we have to attend his Change of Command ceremony. That's right: We've been ordered to risk our lives to attend a Dog and Pony Show.

Oh, we've tried like hell to get out of it. But, this is a big deal in a commander's career; I've had two of them, myself. I just didn't order people to get shot at in order to attend. But, the show must go on

We only have less than two months before we redeploy, and we're about to play chicken with the Grim Reaper so that Colonel Buzzkill can feel good about himself. My knuckles are white as they clutch my M-16, and my eyes are wide open, scanning the trash alongside the road.

Is it that cardboard box?

Is it the depression on the shoulder, marked by freshly turned earth?

I feel a powerful urge to shoot at these anomalies along our path; maybe I can detonate the bomb BEFORE it gets us. That would be insane, but it might work. I'm past the point of caring whether anything I do gets me in trouble. I only want us to go home alive. Colonel Buzzkill isn't making that any easier.

A few miles down the road, we come to an abrupt halt. The security forces patrolling ROUTE IRISH have found an IED up ahead.

Of course, they have! What else would they find along this piece of shit road?

Colonel Herriot calls ahead to tell our brigade HQ the situation The answer is not long in coming: Find another route. We'll wait for you.

How considerate!

Abbas, our interpreter, tells us he can find a way through southern Baghdad to the palace complex. The area is predominately Shiite. They resent Americans because we're Americans. At the end of Desert Storm, Americans promised the Shiites they would be supported if they rose up against Saddam. Thousands of Shiites staged an uprising in southern Iraq. We didn't follow through, and Saddam exterminated them. Hoping the Shiites in Baghdad have short memories, we start out on the detour.

Meandering through slums, we make our way. We're passing a herd of sheep in a lot between the houses, when SFC Wilkes calls out: "Oh, look at the pretty lambs!"

"Yeah, Sergeant," I think to myself. "There's probably an insurgent with an AK-47 or an RPG saying the same thing about us. Keep scanning your sector!" I yell across the HUMVEE at her.

Eventually, we make it to the palace and its relative safety. We withstand a thirty minute Change of Command ceremony, endure small talk with a few generals and VIPs, drink chai and munch on baklava, and clamber into our HUMVEES for the trip home.

Again, about half way there, we are forced to stop. A quick call confirms the incredible but inevitable: there's an IED up ahead. We need to find an alternate route, or we will be driving ROUTE IRISH in darkness. And that is something you just don't even contemplate; it's that bad.

I look over at Abbas; he's got his map out. He smiles and tells me that once again, he's found a detour.

Love that man…

This time, we thread our way through the northwestern area of Baghdad known as Al Mansour. It's predominately made up of Sunni Iraqis, who resent us because we toppled their benefactor, Saddam, not quite a year ago. The detour is uneventful. We approach Checkpoint One near BIAP. Traffic is at a standstill, so I get out of my HUMVEE, which is the trail vehicle in our column of unwilling Baghdad tourists. A convoy of flatbed trucks is delivering large double-wide trailers to Camp Victory. These will be the living quarters for hundreds of troops who will be stationed on that FOB. There's an entrance to Victory off of ROUTE IRISH, and one of the trailers is stuck in the stone gate, impeding any forward progress into BIAP. This time, we can't make a detour; there are dozens of US military and Iraqi vehicles around us. To our right is a guardrail.

We are stuck in traffic, in a combat zone.

I climb back into my vehicle to wait this out. A few US soldiers with bomb-sniffing dogs are walking between the Iraqis' cars. A Toyota van filled with Iraqi workers sits directly to my left. Suddenly, one of the German Shepherds sits down right in front of the van, and begins barking like crazy.

"Aw, c'mon! Not this bullshit, again!" I'm more indignant than scared. This is just getting old fast.

As it turns out, the German shepherd alerted for no reason; there were no explosives in the van or on any of the Iraqis. Bad dog, no biscuit!

As we finally make it back to the Crack House, I make the prediction that the Baghdad Airport Road will become known as the most dangerous highway in the world. Sometimes, I hate being right.

Back to the World

The convoy leaves the highway and pulls into the vast, crushed stone parking lot on BIAP's west side. Soldiers park their HUMVEES and trucks in long lines, sending up billowing clouds of white stone dust.

The dust is one of the two reasons I have a massive headache. It irritates the hell out of my nasal passages and sinus cavities. The other reason for the throbbing in my temple is the arrival of this particular Army Reserve unit.

They are the soldiers of our parent Civil Affairs brigade, which has inhabited the Puzzle Palace in the Green Zone for the past ten months. We are finally redeploying to Kuwait, and then home. Unfortunately, these guys will accompany us.

Over the past eleven months, the officers and senior NCOs of this brigade have been the bane of our existence. While we've lived in an abandoned building during that time (being quartered in something called the "Crack House" has got to the ultimate symbol of roughing it), these straphangers have had a cushy life living and working in one of Saddam's palaces. The first three months of our tour, we ate MREs and food scrounged from other units. They ate in a huge dining facility at which diplomats and other VIP's enjoyed their meals.

Back then, after we had exhausted our supply of MREs, I'd called down to their Brigade Supply Officer and requested more. He told me, "Oh, we don't have any of those down here." I replied, sarcastically, "Are you for real? What are you guys living on down there: berries and live frogs?"

They also seldom left the safety of the Green Zone; therefore, they are recognized as the original Fobbits. This fact is the salient reason why my blood pressure is now skyrocketing.

The Brigade Sergeant Major and a few of his cronies are busy chewing out our soldiers, because our battalion vehicles have not been steam-cleaned, and the tires have not been rubbed with Armor-All. Several of our HUMVEES are also dented and sport bullet holes.

"What the fuck do they think we've been doing for the past eleven months!" I ask Colonel Herriot. "You mean to tell me they don't know all the work we've been doing?"

He replies that he knows how ridiculous the situation is, but he just wants to get out of Iraq and go home. Arguing with these morons will only make our time with them even more intolerable.

A solitary figure walks quickly across the lot toward me. It's LTC Winston, the cheery good old boy from North Carolina, who'd been sent to help us in the aftermath of that bloody week last July. He'd been a welcome addition to our team, and worked hard to make sure our operations passed the Common Sense Test. A month ago, LTC Winston had returned to the Puzzle Palace, and we'd been very sorry to see him go.

LTC Winston doesn't look cheery now. He rips off his Kevlar and throws it into the dust.

"Damn those birdbrains! We're two hours late 'cuz those idiots fucked up our convoy on the way out here! We had to pull over twice on ROUTE IRISH to get reorganized!"

"Sir, what do you mean you pulled over? That's not something you do on that road! That's not Interstate 95. They call it "Ambush Alley" for good reason!"

I can't believe it! We're about to drive 350 miles through the Badlands of southern Iraq with these clowns, and they've fucked up moving just the eight miles to get out here!

We're doomed. We won't make it out of Iraq alive, if they're along with us.

My death and those of my soldiers are virtually a reality.

The next morning, we start for Kuwait along MSR Tampa.

Our first objective is Camp Cedar II, a refueling point not too far from where we stopped on our way up to Baghdad. That was ten months ago, but it seems more like ten years.

We arrive at Cedar II an hour before dusk, and commence refueling. The word spreads like wildfire around the parked vehicles: another convoy has been hit by an IED at an overpass barely twenty minutes after we go by. The attack has occurred in broad daylight, which means the device had been in place as we'd passed through; the insurgents plant them at night to avoid detection. Why the triggerman has spared us remains a mystery. At this point, I see that particular insurgent as less of an enemy than I do these jokers with whom we're traveling. Pretty sad, huh?

A truck has taken the full brunt of the IED, but there are no casualties. The incident serves as a glaring reminder that we're not out of the woods, yet. Not by a long shot.

The next day, we pass through the border into Kuwait. Everybody pulls over on the highway past the checkpoint. We get out of the HUMVEES and congratulate each other on having made it out of Iraq, alive. Myself, I don't completely relax. We still have to get on a plane and make it across the Atlantic; but at least, our fate now rests in the hands of the cockpit crew, and not these weirdos.

Shannon Airport: The Emerald Isle.

Our second stop on our long journey home after leaving Kuwait. It's about 0330 when we land to refuel; that's no surprise since it always seems to be Oh Dark 30 every time we land to refuel the humongous L-1011 jumbo jet.

The duty free shop and pub are closed, of course. The airport manager offers to call in the staff so that our troops can drink, but the major tasked with ensuring the soldiers get back on the plane refuses the kind gesture. Colonel Herriot and another high-ranking officer strongly urge him to change his mind. They win.

Now, it's only been a couple months since I've had a drink; I'd gone home on leave in December-January. But I can't pass up a couple of pints of Guinness in the land of my forefathers. That would be heresy! My fellow passengers agree, and are busy drinking pints and buying out the whiskey inventory at the duty free shop.

Back on the plane, the passenger who's been my aisle companion since Kuwait has disappeared. In his place is a young, very inebriated sergeant. I'm pretty well lit up, myself.

Who is this guy? I've never seen him before. And, where did that captain I was talking to go? I hope he got back on the plane!

My new buddy, the sergeant, is conducting a chemistry experiment involving a 2-liter bottle of Pepsi, and a fifth of Jameson's. It sits in the aisle next to his seat. He takes a long swig and turns to me.

"I luff you guys!"

Never seen this guy before.

"You guys are the best! Luff you guys!" he tells me emphatically. His breath has an octane rating, and I'm glad this is a non-smoking flight.

A flight attendant notices his bottle on the carpet. She bends down and tells him, "Sir, you're going to have to put that away."

"Aw, that's not gonna be a problem!" He upends the plastic bottle and guzzles noisily.

Our plane drops out of the clouds, and prepares to touch down again on American soil. Its wheels hit the tarmac at Pope Air Force Base, North Carolina, the same field we'd started our journey one year ago, a year in which every one of us has changed forever. A cheer roars through the cabin as we celebrate passing the true litmus test of finally being home.

We leave the L-1011 and march in formation to a hangar, where an official welcoming party awaits. There's a 3 star general, a band, and a crowd of cheering civilians. We're ordered to the position of attention as the band plays the Star Spangled Banner.

Oh, man, this could be bad! I'm still pretty drunk, suffering from jet lag, no sleep, and an overdose of coffee on the plane. It feels like we're standing here forever. When did the National Anthem turn into Free Bird?

We're in the middle of our post deployment physical at Fort Bragg. Obviously, the Army wants to determine if we have any physical ailments or injuries as a result of our year in Iraq.

One of the troops has Crohn's Disease, a painful affliction of the bowel. A year ago, in this same medical facility, the Army doctors had cleared him for deployment. They had told him that he would be fine as long as he was taking ant-inflammatory drugs, which they had told him would be readily available in Iraq. I'm at a loss of how they could predict that, but in any case, there was none.

An Army doctor reads his medical chart and becomes incensed that this soldier was deployed even though he had Crohn's Disease.

"This is unconscionable!" he declares. "Who medically cleared this soldier to deploy? I want his name and rank!"

Another doc checks the signature on the deployment record from a year ago.

"Uh, you did, Sir."

There's hardly any emphasis on the psychological effects of our deployment; it'll be years before that goes under the microscope. There is a very, very short questionnaire that has to be filled out. Most of the questions are inane: "Do you have thoughts of harming yourself and others?" "Did you have unprotected sex during your deployment?"

And my personal favorite: Did you see dead people?"

"Nah! You never see those in combat."

For now, we're poked, prodded, and herded into and out of buildings. One of many medical procedures that we have to endure is blood drawing.

A long line of recently redeployed soldiers stands in a hallway. Every few minutes, a gruff voice calls out, "Next!" from a small room at the end of the corridor. Periodically, we hear curses and exclamations of pain come from the room.

What the hell is going on?

"Don't you know how to find a vein, you dumbass?" A sergeant storms from the room, clutching his forearm. The Army specialist drawing blood needs more training, as he continually misses the soldiers' veins, striking the muscle and bone with his needles.

Now, it's my turn. I walk into the office and sit down at a desk. The specialist is already working on the forearm of an attractive blonde female soldier. He's trying to hit on her while he's working, but she's not biting.

"So, how many guys wrote you love letters while you were in Iraq", he asks, smiling at her.

"My boyfriend wrote me emails every day," she says, watching the needle going into her arm.

Casanova-now fishing for sympathy-stops grinning and says, "I've been deployed here for six months, and nobody's written me."

"Listen, asshole," she tells him. "You're not deployed! You're stationed here. Only soldiers who serve overseas are 'deployed.' Stop saying that shit, right damn now!"

The medical tech is absolutely shocked this would come from

the lips of such a sweet-looking girl. But you figure she's probably seen some bad things. And she's not finished; she delivers the coup de grace.

"And you hurt people! Who the hell would want to write you?" she asks coldly.

A raucous cheer erupts from the hallway.

Another line; this one's at the Clothing Issue Facility (CIF). We're here to turn in all the gear that was issued to us before we deployed. The Army wants all its gear given back to it in the same or better condition than when it left. There is no tolerance for dirty or damaged gear, no matter which combat zone you've just survived.

One of our soldiers has already been through this. Yesterday, he attempted to turn in an olive green duffle bag. The civilians at the CIF, who work for the Department of Defense, had rejected it, even though he'd just cleaned it. So now, he's back with a brand new one he bought at an Army-Navy store off post. Based on the shouting that reaches my ears, things are not going well today, either.

I move up to the front to find out what's happening. The soldier's big mistake is that he's removed the bag from its plastic wrapper. The civilian has just declared it to be dirty. Any normal person would be annoyed. After all we've been through, I can't just stand there and take this.

"Are you kidding me? That's a brand new bag he's brought in! There's no way in Hell it could have gotten dirty."

"Hey, can't you read? There is no profanity allowed in this facility, soldier!"

My eyes follow his index finger to a white placard with bold black lettering on the wall:

NO PROFANITY ALLOWED!
ZERO TOLERANCE

VIOLATORS WILL BE REPORTED TO THEIR COMMANDER

This is laughable.

In the Army, swearing is just as natural as breathing. Our team has just finished a deployment during which people tried very hard to kill us; we've raised swearing to an art form.

"Listen, buddy. Our commander is at the back of this line, and you've probably forgotten the profanity he'll use when he hears about this, uh, crap!"

My bluff fails: the colonel ends up getting in trouble, too.

Utter bullshit! Whoops!

WARNING:
THIS BOOK CONTAINS PROFANITY

KEEP OUT OF REACH OF DEPARTMENT OF DEFENSE CIVILIANS EMPLOYED AT ARMY CLOTHING ISSUE FACILITIES.

THE "F WORD" MAKES THEM CRY

Mandatory Fun

"The beatings will continue until morale improves."

-Standard Operating Procedure in most US Army units

So, we're sitting on our asses in Camp Doha, waiting impatiently for the word to get on a plane to go back to The World. By this time, I'm completely disenchanted with our brigade staff who've tagged along on the long haul from Baghdad to Kuwait City. These people can't get out of their own way.

About three days after we arrive in Kuwait, someone in the Supply Section realizes they are missing approximately $725,000 worth of equipment they are responsible for. Most of the missing items are secure communications radios. Now, maybe they aren't actually missing, but each piece of equipment in the military is supposed to be present; if not, then there had better be a piece of paper documenting its location or status. These bozo's have neither. After that 360 mile drive south from Baghdad, after all that bullshit, the Headquarters Company Commander, who is personally responsible for the gear, has to go ALL the way back to Baghdad to locate the stuff. This is no simple task; it isn't like turning around on your way to work to check if you've turned off the iron. Southern Iraq was now No Man's Land, The Great Unknown; insurgents were sowing IEDs like dandelions all along MSR Tampa.

The new commander, Colonel Buzzkill, is irate about this and other incidents that have happened since he has taken command two months ago. His staff is clearly not working together. By now, he's probably thinking a deployment under his belt and a Bronze Star on his chest may not be worth all of this horseshit. He comes up with a plan to build unit cohesion.

Colonel Buzzkill drops the bombshell that there is no camaraderie amongst his officers. So, he orders us to participate in a volleyball tournament.

Now, my first reaction, besides shock, is that if you're not able to build camaraderie and unit cohesion during 10 months in a combat zone, I really don't think organized sports will fit the bill. But, of course, I'm a team player, so I figure that it will help pass the time before we finally get on the Freedom Bird.

I'm in the first match of the Mandatory Fun Invitational. I'm also the first to serve. I suck at volleyball; absolutely horrid at organized sports as a whole. The only thing in volleyball I don't suck at is serving. The first couple of times I serve the ball, it actually makes it over the net, surprising everyone, including me.

Our team begins to practice and it's painful to watch. Colonel Quickdraw is on my team and he's positioned right in front of me. Even with his thick Birth Control Glasses, he's blind as a bat. He's also less athletic than me. The entire time we're practicing, he's never quite able to keep his eye on the ball. No matter where the ball goes, Quickdraw is out of synch; it's like watching a tape delay inside a tape. He just keeps whirling around in his own little game. It's then that I decide Quickdraw invented disco.

The first match: oh how exciting! I wind up and hit the ball over the net. To my dismay, it goes right to the bodybuilder, Adonis. He spikes-no, he launches-the ball upward. It hits the gym ceiling with an audible Whap and streaks down toward me. I put my hands together to spike it in self-defense, but I'm just a little bit too slow. The volleyball hits my left thumb at full force.

Shit, that hurt!

My thumb smarts, my hand is numb, and my arm begins twitching of its own accord, but the match must go on. Now, I'm not even playing; I'm in a defensive posture, trying to hit the ball with my right hand while my left is doing Tourette's.

"Use both hands to spike!" yells Colonel Quickdraw.

No shit! Didn't you see me try that! On second thought, you probably didn't....

By now, I'm begging for a substitute to take my place. I'm finally removed from the game, and seek out our PA, CPT Hammond, for medical attention. He tells me that my thumb is broken.

Broken! I survive eleven months of dodging rockets and barely avoiding friendly fire, and my thumb gets broken in a volleyball match just before I return home. Forgetting that there's an eight-hour time difference, I call my friend, Bob, who works in Officer Recruiting back at my old unit. It's 3am back in the States as he awakens and asks me groggily why I've called. I tell him that the people I'm with are dirt stupid, and that I want to join the National Guard Witness Protection Program.

The War at Home

Memorial Day 2004

I'm at the parade in my hometown; American flags, horns and bagpipes fill the air. Crowds line the streets. Cars filled with dignitaries and veterans of our country's wars sit lined up, ready to start the parade. As a young boy, I've seen it dozens of times.

This time, it's different: now, I'M one of the veterans. And, yes, it feels very, very surreal.

The parade starts. My family and friends are here. I'm supposed to be throwing candy to the kids, but I'm so nervous, it's all I can do to wave and flash a plastic smile every 10 seconds. I just want this to be over.

Now, don't get me wrong: I'm honored to be here. But, I have to let you know this parade is the only one in the country where the real parade is on the sidewalk, and the spectators are moving down the street. There are hundreds of-let's put it this way-colorful people lining the sidewalks. Nice people, but they're a crowd, and crowds make me nervous.

Suddenly, I catch movement in my peripheral vision. There's a figure running fast toward me on the right. I cringe. He's wild-eyed and drunk, and looks very....earthy. The kind of guy who has a riflescope on his chainsaw. Get my drift?

I've never really liked anyone running toward me while I'm in a car. I REALLY don't like it now.

When I was in Iraq, the Navy SEALS gave our Civil Affairs soldiers training on maneuvering through the civilian populace and being secure. One tidbit was "We know that part of your job is to smile and wave. But first, look at their hands. Because the hands will tell you everything you need to know: look closely and make double damn sure they're not holding weapons, detonators, or grenades. Then, and only then, you should look them in the eye, smile and wave."

Mr. Drunk Guy-sans weapons, detonators, or grenades-skids to a halt beside the convertible. He raises his hand and brings it down, presumably to give me a High Five. But I'm not really in the mood, so I sit there, still anticipating something bad. His hand connects with the side view mirror. Slowly, his sloshed brain registers pain.

"OW!"

Then, leaning in so close I can tell what he used the beer to wash down, he yells:

"Now, go back over there and kick their ass!!!"

No, you put the beer down and go over there and kick their ass! I'm done with all that. Who do you think I am, your war bitch?

Parades will never be the same for me: I've lost my innocence.

My Reflexes Are The Bomb!

There is a silver lining to spending a year dodging high explosive rockets: you develop strong self-preservation skills.

Back home, I have a greater ability to sense danger; I often feel like I've placed a safety zone around me. When you feel like someone or something is getting close to penetrating that cushion, you become hyper-vigilant.

I find myself anticipating someone walking around a blind corner toward me. I tense up automatically, worried that I'll bump into an elderly woman carrying 16 bags of groceries, and ruin her week.

I'm at a gas station, filling up at the island, on the way home from National Guard weekend.

Man, the price of gas went up again! I thought all that Iraqi oil was supposed –

BOOM!!!!

I'm face down, sprawled on the concrete, wondering how I got here. I look to the right and see a Harley. It backfired. It wasn't an IED or a grenade. Standing up and dusting myself off, I notice people staring at me. A woman glances at my uniform and remarks, "Ah."

Explains everything.

At least they're not laughing, I think to myself.

Loud noises like backfires, crowds, hunters bagging a deer, champagne bottles uncorking, Billy Mays, and supermarket announcements: these are a few of my least favorite things.

It's gotten better in the nine years I've been back, but they can still get me shaking in my boots.

Fireworks? No way! There are three things I am deathly afraid of:
1. Fire
2. Bullets
3. Fire that acts like a bullet

On the Fourth of July, if my friends can't find me, they just look down.

When I'm stuck in traffic or construction, the first thing that springs into my mind is not: I'm going to be late for work; more like: This spot would make one pisser of an ambush!

I'm not really sure why my friends insist on attending the New York State Fair. The experience reminds me of parts of Baghdad: unbearably hot, smells like garbage, the crush of thousands of people. The two times I've gone to the Fair since my deployment, I had to drink like a madman in order to escape the flashbacks. Baghdad even has a Midway; every trip there is a scary ride.

Convicted felons should be bussed to the State Fair. That should be a good crime deterrent. Inmates on Death Row should be forced to judge the hog competition.

I'm on Interstate 81 north of Syracuse. At one point, it becomes three lanes. My car is in the center lane. Suddenly, a dump truck comes barreling up on my left, which is enough to raise my guard. Then, the sucker backfires.

Oh, shit…

I take evasive action in my Honda Civic. I swerve to the right, away from the threat, nearly sideswiping a sedan. Now on the right shoulder, heart pumping, I start mentally yelling at the gunner in the turret.

"ACTION LEFT!!

"SUPPRESSIVE FIRE!!"

"LIKE NOW, WE'RE TAKING FIRE, DAMMIT!!"

Wait. I don't have a turret; I don't even have a damn sunroof!

What the hell is wrong with me?

As the adrenaline rush subsides, I slip back into reality, and notice that my fellow motorists are asking the same thing. Horns are blaring and people are letting me know they think I'm "Number One".

"As if I meant to do that! To hell with ANYBODY who doesn't deal with this shit!"

"God, how long will this go on?"

I've since learned there are some things you should NOT ask out loud.

The Barley Field

Now's a REALLY bad time to reach muscle failure.

I'm willing my legs to churn through the calf-deep mud, but even the possibility of getting shot with an assault rifle, or disemboweled by a mortar burst won't do the trick. The muddy field, recently plowed and sowed, has soaked up several inches of rain in the last few days. It's a quagmire.

Rain. Who'd of thought it would rain in this arid shithole? Strange as it may seem, this thought is competing with my survival instinct for space in my brain as I run (or give it my best effort) for my life.

I can almost taste the irony of my predicament: It's less than a month before we're scheduled to redeploy. We're at the tail end of one of our last rebuilding projects. The mosque west of the airport is finally finished, and everyone-our battalion, the local villagers, the contractors, the Imam, the Army photographers and reporters- have all come together to celebrate with a Grand Reopening ceremony. Tables of food are filled with a feast: hummus, rice, lamb, falafel, you name it. A shame it will all get cold.

The massive ground attack we've all dreaded has finally come to pass. A few minutes ago, we'd been startled by heavy small arms fire, muffled by distance but still scary as hell. Then, the radio had crackled to life with the report:

"Contact! Gate Seven!"

"All stations this net: BIAP Gate Seven is taking small arms and indirect fire! Gate Seven is closed! I say again, Gate Seven is closed!"

The attackers are between us and the airport: The Sanctuary.

The celebrants, frozen at first by the sound of the rifle reports, have scattered. Most of the Iraqis can't understand English, but they can tell something is up. The insurgents will definitely seek retribution for collaborating with Americans.

We sprint toward our HUMVEEs, only to discover they are parked nowhere the mosque. The Trained Killer, by this time especially paranoid and terrified because he's so close to leaving for good, has ordered the drivers to park out on the roadway, presumably to make a fast getaway in the likelihood of an attack. An attack that is actually happening right now.

More rifle shots, followed by muffled, but unmistakable sounds in the distance: THOONK! THOONK! Mortars leaving their tubes. It's only a matter of time before the Bad Guys figure out the range, and then they'll catch us in the open.

To get to the vehicles, we have to traverse the muddy field. The muck is creating a terrible suction on our boots. Everyone is moving in short, jerky movements in order to escape the pull on our boots, our knees pumping up and down unnaturally. A mortar round impacts a few meters in back of Big D. Through a spray of mud and water, I watch him land face down in Iraqi real estate.

Those motherfuckers! They killed him! I have the urge to spin around and open fire on the insurgents dropping the rounds, but I can't see through the mud in my eyes.

Incredibly, Big D regains his footing and, huge legs churning the mud, makes it to his HUMVEE.
It would take a small army to take him down.

I'm utterly exhausted. We all are. My lungs are burning, and my heart is pumping so fast I can only feel one continuous, ragged thrum.

"Major Ready! Keep going! You're almost there!"

The rest of the troops are at the vehicles. Most of them have taken cover behind the armor plate bolted on by the Iraqi machinists three months ago. Each HUMVEE looks like a tan porcupine with black quills protruding from its hide.

I'm the last one. It's only ten yards up an earthen berm to my vehicle, but it might just as well be ten miles. I can't go any further. So, this is where it ends. I'm gonna die in a cold, muddy field eight time zones from home.

My small radio, fastened to my Kevlar helmet, shrieks in my ear: "Peacemaker 5! Keep going! They're waiting for you!"

I don't know who's calling me on the radio, but I want to call them back and tell them it's too late for me, and to leave me. I think of my two young sons and begin sobbing.

"Patrick! Michael! I'm so sorry! I tried, but I can't go any farther!"

"Daddy! What's wrong?"

"What?" The mud releases its hold on my boots, and my breathing and heartbeat have slowed.

"Dad, you were screaming and crying like crazy. Did you have a bad dream? You OK?"

My eyes fly open. I'm soaking wet, sweat running down my face. Sitting up in bed, I glance toward the bedroom door at two pairs of widened eyes, staring at me in shock from the dark.

Sighing, my head drops to the soaked pillow. I'm overcome with relief. Tumbling out of bed, I walk toward my boys and hug them to me.

"Yeah. Daddy had a bad dream, but it's over."

Thank You for Your Service. Now Get To Work!

"Those who do not do battle for their country, do not know with what ease they accept their citizenship in America." --Dean Brelis, "The Face of South Vietnam"

No memoir of combat would be complete without a discussion of what happens when soldiers return home to the civilian world. As you are about to read, this period is as much part of war as the bullets and bombs. Often, it's worse.

The transition from military to civilian life is difficult enough in peacetime. The experience of combat is an amalgam of emotions and awakenings that make homecoming even more stressful. Over there, even the most junior soldier has a tremendous responsibility no civilian could begin to imagine. The lives of their buddies are in their hands; this experience creates a bond between soldiers that cannot be broken. Back home, only people in the fire service or law enforcement have that kind of loyalty to another human being.

The media hasn't done a very good job of portraying combat veterans. In the past several years, there have been numerous cases of mass murder in the US. On at least three of those occasions, the mainstream media was too quick to run with rumors that the shooters were vets of Iraq or Afghanistan. These rumors were false, of course, but reporters should focus more on getting their facts straight before they go on camera. There's a perception among the media and some Americans, that we are always just a hair's breath away from firing up a Wal-Mart, or ambushing Meals On Wheels.

My company has offered me the job I'd had before Iraq, with no loss in seniority. The owners and the executives are very gracious and accommodating, and have supported me throughout the entire ordeal. They had no issue with me taking sixty days before returning after active duty. The only thing different is that I have another boss, a young woman who I've worked with previously. She outlines my job duties and her expectations, So far, so good.

Carrie tells me that her department prides itself on being a team, and that if there was a project deadline to meet, I could be asked to pitch in on tasks that were not in my job description. "No sweat!" I tell her. After all, I'd been doing just that for an entire year.

In spite of this pep rally, I find myself sitting idly in my cubicle, staring wistfully at Google Map images of Baghdad International Airport.

Two weeks go by. It's a Friday afternoon, almost quitting time, and I'm excited to pick up my two young sons so that we can spend the weekend together. My co-worker, Barb, calls me over to her cubicle. She hands me a thick spiral-bound manual, and drops the bomb that she is leaving the next morning to train at a customer site. She needs twenty copies of it, sorted, collated, and stapled, before she leaves.

The room turns dark. I take the book in my hands and stare at it like it was a collection of satanic verses.

It's like I never left. They expect me to just pick up my life where it left off.

To be fair, I'd promised I would help whenever I could. But when the opportunity actually comes up, it seems so irrelevant, compared to what I'd been doing only a few months before.

The fact that I've been through so much, had my life in someone else's hands, held theirs in mine, means nothing to her. She expects me to do this right now, just before I'm supposed to leave to get my boys. That's an even bigger slap in the face. The time spent with my children is so precious after being apart for what seemed like ages; I've actually missed Mike's birthday two years in a row.

I hand the manual back to her. Staring with contempt through the middle of her face, I finally speak. My voice cracks out of rage and disappointment, as I let her know just how much I appreciate being part of "the team."

"I hope that works out for ya." I turn on my heel and walk toward the exit.

Me and this job are no longer a good fit.

Several months after my return home, a friend invites me to visit his business in Downtown Syracuse. He introduces me to one of his business partners, a tall, attractive woman. She comes from a modestly wealthy family that owns a large dairy. My friend has already told her that I'd been in Iraq.

"Thank you for your service," she tells me. I decide that she's pretty hot.

"Now, you don't have to go back, right?" she asks.

"Actually, I'm still in the National Guard. They could call me up and send me back, sure."

"Wow", she says.
"I don't think my family would ever hire anyone in the National Guard or Reserves. I mean, because you have to be gone so often."

"You're no longer hot," I almost say out loud.

I shake her hand, politely excuse myself, and walk out of her office.

"You can't have it both ways, lady!" I think to myself. "You want me to protect your privileged, silver spoon way of life. But you'd resent the time I'd spend away from work, doing just that."

"Shit! I have more respect for the antiwar movement; at least they believe in something."

I'm stuck at a desk job, doomed to live out the remainder of my working life in quiet desperation. There is no relevance, no sense of immediacy to my work. After working in combat conditions, forced to be constantly vigilant and proactive, knowing that others' lives and the security of another country are at stake, what the hell do you do for an encore?

Steve walks in and awakens me from my miserable daydream. He's a salesman at my company, and a local politician. He is in danger of not meeting his monthly quota. I don't really care for him; he's a bit of a dolt. My nickname for him is Water Baby.

"You were in the military, right?" he asks.

"Yeah, I was in the Reserves." He already knows that. Where's this going?

"Well, my sales numbers are down, and the president is threatening to let me go if they don't improve. So, I started talking with military recruiters. I have half a mind to escape all this bullshit, sell the house, my cars, and my bike, and join up. There's a good chance I would go to Iraq or Afghanistan."

"Yep," I say. "You're tracking. We're at war. If you join the military, you'll be going to war."

"Absolutely! I don't feel like my life is going anywhere. It would be good character building."

I went to war, and I still don't feel like my life is going anywhere. I keep this to myself, merely answering "Yep. Builds character."

Water Baby says, "Plus, it doesn't feel right for me to be an elected official without having served my country."

Maybe I've been wrong about him. I've been saying all along that our appointed and elected leaders should have military experience. Water Baby may actually have a clue.

But, of course, he snaps out of it.

"I'm thirty-six now, and the only branch that will take me is the Army

Reserve. But they won't make me an officer, because I only have an associate's degree. Which is total bullshit, because I think rank should be awarded based on life experience."

My God, he didn't actually say that.

"No, Steve. That's the Salvation Army."

The joke flies right over his head. "I'm seriously considering enlisting. Now, I don't have a death wish. But suppose I go over, get in a firefight, and pull a John Wayne or an Audie Murphy."
This guy's dumber than a box of hair.

"Steve," I say slowly. "Don't try to draw fire. It irritates the people around you."

What mortal sin did I commit, what taboo did I break, to end up working with a boob like this guy?

Bitter, Party of One: Your Table's Ready!

All that is necessary for the triumph of evil is that good men do nothing.
-Attributed to Edmund Burke, Irish political philosopher

During our deployment, our troops were wounded and friends killed, not necessarily because of decisions made in the White House or the Pentagon. War is war, no matter where and how it's waged. The calamities that happened to our tiny detachment were due to a lot of stupid people in our chain of command making stupid decisions. I made more than my share of them.

Some of the decisions made at the national and global level could be described as criminal.

Al-Faw Palace, northeast of the Airport: a sprawling, literally palatial estate built by Saddam Hussein to commemorate the victory over Iran decades ago. This complex contains over 62 rooms and 29 bathrooms. Like everything else in Iraq, Saddam built it really as a monument to himself than a national victory. The buildings surrounded a huge, man-made lake.

I call it "Six Flags Over Baghdad".

At first sight, this palace, and the other 74 built throughout Iraq seem spectacular, even beautiful. When you realize where the money came from to make it happen, it's an obscenity.

After Desert Storm, the United Nations imposed economic sanctions on Iraq, in order to keep Saddam from expanding his military and deter further aggression on his part. He cried poverty, and begged the UN to allow him to sell a portion of his oil to buy food and medicine for the Iraqi people. It was called the "UN Oil-for-Food Program, and for a time was administered by the son of a Secretary-General.

Saddam was able to divert most of the revenue from its intended purpose. Thousands of Iraqis died as a result. The palaces were built with blood money. I guess somebody at the UN looked the other way.

For the most part, the mainstream American media was on-board with the White House before and during the invasion of Iraq in March 2003. It was a big story, and the pesky squabble over Weapons of Mass Destruction muddied the waters. Like the White House, the media had "Go Fever".

Once that it was apparent that Saddam didn't have these weapons, and wasn't behind 9/11, the darlings of the media establishment wasted no time hitching their wagons to a new star. The new theme was that America was doomed to fail in Iraq. As soon as it became apparent that the invasion was ill conceived, the debate in Congress and in the news should have ended right there. Now that we were in Iraq, Americans needed to work together, to show the enemy, and the world that we would accept nothing less than victory. We needed a unity of purpose like that during World War II.

As it turns out, the only people who were united and fighting for a common goal were our servicemen and women. Some things never change.

The civilian contractor is talking my ear off as I wait for a haircut. He's bragging about the sweetheart deal that's brought him to Iraq: a five year gig with a defense contractor; he only has to work in Iraq for one year, then he's off to Brazil. The contract guarantees him a salary of $87,000 a year.

He drives a bus.

Now, don't get me wrong: driving any vehicle anywhere in Iraq is dangerous. But my new friend's route is confined to the interior of BIAP, where he merely runs the risk of mortar and rocket attacks. His Army counterparts, men and women holding the rank of sergeant, are paid a mere fraction of the civilian's salary. And, they have to drive on ROUTE IRISH.

Call me simple, but maybe the money we're throwing at the contractor would best be used to bolster the paychecks of these brave servicemen and women. At the very least, it would show that their country values their service and sacrifice more than filling corporate coffers.

Today's military is an all-volunteer force; there is no draft. The American soldier serves his country for any number of reasons. It could be out of a sense of duty and patriotism, or the promise of money for a college education. She may join because military service runs in her family.

Regardless of the reason, a serviceman takes an oath and signs a contract for any number of years. In doing so, he writes a check to the American people for the amount up to, and including his life. In return, he is promised, and expects, the proper training, equipment, pay, and the leadership required to do the job. And, that he will be accepted back into the society that sent him to war. That's all he or she wants, in the long run.

When we, as leaders, military and civilian, fail to provide, we are telegraphing to these and future soldiers that we don't have their backs, and that we don't care. Good luck training the Cub Scouts for your next conflict, because that's all you'll have to draw on.

Fort Bragg, NC, March 31, 2004.

The images on the television screen nearly cause me to lose my dinner: the bodies of American security contractors being desecrated by a smiling, enthusiastic mob. Two of the charred corpses are hung from a bridge in Fallujah.

Assholes! Somebody needs to teach these people a lesson!

We've redeployed back to the States, and are just about to leave Active Duty and return home. We started out a year ago on a journey from this same place, filled with enthusiasm for the chance to help people halfway around the globe. Our tiny band has changed, and every one of us is filled with rage at the crowd on the screen.

Fuck these people!

I'd been an infantry officer for years, and had made the transition to a humanitarian role. The video has pushed me back toward the mindset of a warrior. I remember concocting a vengeful plan while I sat watching the news in the lounge.

Drop leaflets on the city of Fallujah, warning the population that they had 72 hours to vacate. Why 72? Nice even number.

Anybody left in the city after the deadline is stupid, illiterate, or an insurgent. Invite the American and international media to record what comes next. We're trying to send a message here.

Drop a GBU-43 MOAB (Massive Ordnance Air Blast, aka Mother of All Bombs). This thermobaric weapon has a yield of 11 tons. It's considered the most powerful non-nuclear device ever made. Anybody within a mile will undergo a significant emotional experience, and a catastrophic decrease in fun. And you tell the assembled witnesses:

"This is what happens when you screw with Americans."

To my fellow veterans who disagree with the musings and opinions I've put forth in this book, I respect your right to do so. You earned it.

To any liberals, conservatives, Far Left and Far Right agitators, along with the mainstream media and pundits who profess to educate and inform the American people, while creating controversy in the name of greater ad revenue: I also respect your right to disagree. Remember that, unless you've walked in my shoes, been where I've been, seen what I've seen, you can't judge.

If you fail to respect that, then feel free to play hide and go and fuck yourself.

My Apologies

My life since Iraq has not turned out to be gravy; on the other hand, it's not a cesspool either. There've been a lot of changes; in the way I view my country, and the rest of the world, and myself.

Whereas I'd been very complacent and meek during my life up until that year, now I find myself initially distrustful of authority; I don't follow blindly without questioning. My fuse has gotten a bit shorter, in that I go from zero to asshole in less time than before. When I interact with other people, groups, or the government, my Bullshit-O-Meter is always on. In today's mass media environment, it's almost always pegged.

Until Iraq, questioning authority had never crossed my mind.

Post Traumatic Stress Disorder, survivor guilt, angst, and melancholy. After the Civil War, it was referred to as Soldier's Heart: there are lots of terms that have been pinned to it. Some vets hide it better than others. I tried that: Suck It Up, Grin and Bear It, Be A Man, Ruck Up; you get the idea. I was skeptical before, but I'm here to tell you the shit is real. And it began to eat me up inside.

You're always waiting for the other shoe to drop. Since my return, a number of family emergencies and crises have occurred. Ashamedly, I've met these with the attitude: "Oh, shit! Here we go again!" It's like tilting back in your chair on two legs: that feeling of precarious balance, and then, somebody slams a medicine ball against your chest. Drinking eased the pain a bit in my struggle to quiet an un-quiet mind. The angst and depression came flooding back the next day. This is no way to live your life. I'd been given a second chance, and I was squandering it.

I'd spent half of my life, my entire career, training, planning, anticipating, and awaiting the opportunity to go to war. When it finally happened, it nearly drove me insane.

There's guilt from not acting fast enough, from being complacent, and caving-in to that false sense of security, that arrogance that filled the air once we'd "liberated" Iraq. My gut had told me that it was wrong to follow the crowd. I ignored my instincts. If I hadn't, things may have turned out differently. Maybe it wouldn't have, but it was my responsibility as an officer and a leader to try.

It is one thing to have soldiers you're responsible for wounded and maimed while engaging the enemy. It's quite another for it to happen due to stupid and rash decisions.

All the leadership training and principles I'd let soak into my brain, the absolute truth that a leader is responsible for everything that happens while he's in charge, I took that to heart. The old clichés that "an officer falls on his sword", and "a Captain goes down with the ship", spring from that truth.

Somebody is supposed to take the fall. That's why we're paid the big bucks.

Several months ago, I was writing this book in earnest. The chapters were flying out of my laptop. I was on a roll; my book was finally becoming a reality. After a group session at the local VA, I was talking with another vet in the parking lot. He'd been in Vietnam, had been wounded, and up until that point, hadn't really addressed his PTSD symptoms. He casually asked me where I'd served. I told him that I'd been in Iraq. His next words knifed through my soul.

"I lost my son in Iraq," he said.

There was now a lead weight in my gut. I couldn't talk. Hopefully, he could see how sorry I was; right then, I was paralyzed with fear, sorrow and dread.

I don't remember starting my car. Driving away, the tears began to come. Soon, my vision was so badly blurred, I pulled over.

Here was a guy who'd been through war decades ago, and like myself, he had unresolved issues. Now, he was dealing with the loss of a child, too. It had somehow escaped me that more than one tragedy could happen to a single human being. My sorrow for him washed over me. Next came the fear: fear that something similar could happen to my loved ones, and that I wouldn't have the strength and fortitude that this gentleman had. This new, terrible knowledge of mine changed all the rules of how I was supposed to deal with tragedy.

I didn't start writing again until just a few weeks ago. By the grace of God, my strength has returned.

Fortunately, there is a bright side to all of this: I value my family and friends so much more. I spend a lot more time with my kids; try to laugh more often, and to slow down. There's a greater appreciation of life, amid the knowledge of just how quickly we can leave this world.

I've seen the elephant.

Probably most importantly, I've learned to forgive. I've forgiven those who'd wronged us. Even the Trained Killer gets a pass; he didn't do anything that I wasn't partly guilty of myself. It doesn't mean I condone what they did, but if there's revenge inside your heart, you may as well dig two graves.

I can only hope that others can forgive me.

I believe it's time I wrote The Letters. Of course, letters to the families of our wounded were written and mailed by Colonel Herriot that first week in July 2003. And obviously, the casualty notifications from the Pentagon, the same format for ages:

"The Secretary of the Army has asked me to express his deep regret that your son…"

But these are letters I need to write, because the soldiers' families need to know the real reasons why their loved ones have come home maimed: I wasn't strong enough.

On my iPod is the soundtrack from the Civil War film, "Gods and Generals". The music is dramatic and soothing all at once, which is exactly what I need to accomplish my unfulfilled mission.

I want to drink badly, but there's nothing in the house. There's a blizzard outside and the roads are shitty, so a trip to the liquor store is out of the question. I'll have to find something else to bolster me.

I'd never really been a deeply religious person while growing up. When I was young, church was a place I got in trouble because my siblings and me were always goofing around. As an adult, I didn't do much better: attended church on Sunday, but it was mechanical. But, there's no time like the present.

The Lord is my shepherd; I shall not want.
He makes me to lie down in green pastures: he leads me beside the still waters.

My shoulders slump. I'm overcome by sadness and intense guilt. Even so, I try and buck up; need to finish these letters, after all this time.

Here goes:
   "Dear Mrs. Morrissey, I was your husband's Executive Officer in Iraq…"

"On June 5, 2003, your husband was wounded in action by an Improvised Explosive Device as he and his team left the security of the base perimeter, in order to attend a meeting in the Green Zone, a meeting which served absolutely no fucking purpose. I should have raised the Bullshit Flag and countermanded the orders of our superiors, but couldn't find the courage."

He restores my soul. He leads me in the paths of righteousness. Yea, though I walk through the valley of the shadow of death, I will fear no evil.

I got this; I'm feeling stronger now.

"Dear Mr. and Mrs. Richfield, I was your son's Second-in-Command in Iraq…"

For thou art with me. Thy rod and thy staff comfort me.

"On July 7, 2003, he and his fellow soldiers left the security of the base perimeter in one HUMVEE, in flagrant violation of existing force protection policy. I knew that this would be attempted, but I didn't speak up. Shame on me."

I wish I'd been wounded. Give anything to take this back, to go back to that week in July years ago, and make things right. And have physical wounds to show the pain that is inside me.

The song that's now playing is "Going Home", written and performed by the artist Mary Fahl.

It's a wistful, hopeful song about leaving war to finally come home, something I haven't been able to do mentally. Seems appropriate.

They say there's a place where dreams have all gone.
They never said where, but I think I know.

It's miles through the night, just over the dawn.
On the road that will take me home.

I know in my bones, I've been here before.
The ground feels the same though the land's been torn.

I've a long way to go, the stars tell me so
On this road that will take me home.

And when I pass by, don't lead me astray.
Don't try to stop me! Don't stand in my way.

I remember a friend in Iraq, a sergeant from First Armored, who'd also had a soldier wounded, comparing his intense guilt to an accident in high school. He was 17 and had just gotten his license. One day, a small child on a bike rode out in front of him. His car struck the boy. It wasn't his fault, and the boy eventually recovered. But he remembered that he felt he'd broken a priceless object, something that meant the world to somebody else, and there was no way to take it back.

"This feels like that," he said.

The song seems much louder now, but I haven't touched the volume. Mary's crystal clear, haunting voice nearly drowns out the instruments, as she pulls out all the stops for the next stanza.

Love waits for me 'round the bend, leads me endlessly on.
Surely sorrows shall find their end, and all our troubles will be gone.

Suddenly, after almost a decade, it hits me like a ton of bricks: I need to put this burden down. The enemy pulled the triggers, not me, and blaming myself won't change a thing. And we all came home alive.

And we'll know what we've lost, and all that we've won.
When this road finally takes me home.

I feel the weight leave my shoulders, and where there once was a burden, there's lightness and warmth.

It's time to come home.

Great job, Ms. Fahl…

I'm going home!
I'm going home!
I'm going home!

Head on desk. Sobs.

"I have been driven many times upon my knees by the overwhelming conviction that I had no where else to go."

- Abraham Lincoln

Acknowledgments

"This book would not have been possible...." is one of the biggest clichés in our culture. I use it here in the most genuine and heartfelt manner.

First, I need to thank my Savior, Jesus Christ. You were always with me in the darkest hours of my life, and have guided me in my journey home.

To my two sons, Patrick and Michael Ready, the best sons any father could have. You're the reasons I made it home. Love you!

Singer-songwriter Mary Fahl for graciously allowing me to quote lyrics from her incredibly moving song, "Going Home." This song captures more than any other the feelings and yearnings of a soldier returning from war.

To Dr. Mike Haynie of the Institute for Veterans and Military Families at Syracuse University for writing the foreword.

A very special thanks goes out to my editor, fellow veteran Ron Breland. Thank you for your patience and expertise dealing with my haphazard writing style. You're one of the biggest reasons this book was possible; you are an inspiration.

To Tom Varano, of Varano Photography, thanks for shooting the somewhat disturbing cover photo. Patrick Milmoe and Jeremy Berkey at Canastota Publishing Co., Inc. for their patience and expertise.

To my fellow soldiers of the 414th Civil Affairs Battalion (Forward), 2003-2004: We came, we saw, we made a difference! It was an honor to serve beside such dedicated citizen-soldiers.

To Abbas, our translator and guide, and to our other translators, Faid and Fatima, who put themselves and their families at risk in the service of the United States military: you've done more for this country than most Americans.

Next, my lifelong friend and fellow author, Hank Leo, who has always had my back since we were mere children. Pauline Ingraham, for her marketing expertise, friendship, support and encouragement. Sandy and Terri Leo for their advice.

Melissa Spicer, Melinda Sorrentino, and Steve Kinne, Colonel USAF (Retired), the founders of Clear Path for Veterans: thank you for providing veterans a safe place to make our transition home! I love you guys!

Fellow veterans John R. Mays, Earl Fontenot, Rob Burke, Sean Patrick Galloway, Justin Miller, Terry Finley, and his wife, Teresa. Marine Mom Susan Cannistraro Goodwin. Bill Gandino, for his friendship and guidance in my military career. John-Michael Insetta for his dry wit. My college and ROTC friend from way back, Brian Murphy for his inspiration.

Gold Star Mothers Vicky Barker Arnold, Lorie Schneider and Kathy Ryan Brown: you are pillars of strength.

Fellow veterans and authors, Matt Zeller and Ben Tupper for blazing the literary trail by way of Afghanistan. Oneidans Mark Williams, Tim Rich, and Mary Jane Origlio Roberts for acting as sounding boards, and patiently listening to my stories.

Ria Curley, Esq. for her legal expertise. My nephew, Jack Honis, gets kudos for his proofreading assistance.

I want to thank my parents, Douglas and Sally Ready. Hopefully, this book will help you understand why I've been so quiet since my return. I love you.

Glossary

AK-47: Kalashnikov, 7.62mm automatic weapon. Was the standard weapon of Soviet Bloc soldiers going back decades. Now the preferred armament of discriminating terrorists worldwide.

AWOL: Absent Without Leave; not a good place.

BDU: Battle Dress Uniform; woodland camouflage-patterned clothing worn by American soldiers prior to the Global War on Terror.

BIAP: Baghdad International Airport; formerly Saddam International Airport

Bird: aircraft

Bongo truck: common flat bed truck in Iraq

Chaff- aluminum foil strips ejected from a plane, used to throw off radar-guided surface-to-air missiles (SAM)

C-130 Hercules: 4 propeller cargo aircraft

Dinar: currency of Iraq

DCU-desert camouflage uniform

Dust-Off: Medical evacuation helicopter; in Vietnam, this was the old

UH-1 "Huey" chopper, but has been replaced by the UH-60 Black-hawk. Marked by a red cross on a white background, intended to prevent the enemy from firing on it; the only problem being the new "enemy" doesn't play by those rules. Ass clowns!

Falafel: balls of deep-fried hummus, AKA: Iraqi tater tots

FOB: Forward Operating Base; Army installation in a combat zone, could be very large, like the Green Zone, or a remote outpost.

Fobbit: A serviceman or woman who is stationed on a FOB, and their only time spent "outside the wire", or in danger, is when they arrive and leave. They have cushy jobs.

Green Zone: The area in Downtown Baghdad that was centered on several palaces built by Saddam Hussein's regime. "Green" refers to weapon status Green: weapon on safe, no magazine in weapon, no rounds in the chamber. Considered relatively "safe" except for rocket and mortar attacks, and suicide bombs at the checkpoints.

HDR: Humanitarian Daily Ration. A meal that was developed to be Muslim-friendly. Were meant to be 'gifts from the American people', and handed out to civilians in crisis.

HUMVEE: High Mobility Multipurpose Wheeled Vehicle

(HMMWV) standard transport vehicle of the U.S. military. A Hummer lacking all of the luxuries.

IBA: Interceptor Body Armor; a vest worn by American soldiers (hopefully) containing Kevlar plates designed to stop bullets and shrapnel

IED: Improvised Explosive Device; Any form of mass casualty producing weapon which was not manufactured in a munitions factory or plant

Kevlar: 1.standard helmet of US military 2. Material comprised of layers upon layers of synthetic fibers, which form a fabric; strong but light, very useful in armor applications.

LZ: Landing Zone. An area chosen for helicopters to offload and pickup soldiers and equipment. The pilots appreciate it if the enemy is not in the immediate vicinity.

M-4: 5.56mm carbine. Now the standard weapon of the U.S. military.

MEDEVAC: 1.mode of transportation used to evacuate a casualty to a medical facility; could be a helicopter, plane or ground vehicle; 2.act of evacuating a casualty.

MILES Gear: Multiple Integrated Laser Engagement System: The U.S. military version of Laser Tag. A dramatic improvement over the old days, when we would have to yell "Bang, Bang!"

MRE: Meal Ready to Eat, AKA: Meals Rejected by Ethiopians, Meals Raccoons Enjoy, High octane Puppy Chow. Packaged meals provided to soldiers.

MSR: Main Supply Route. Highway used to transport soldiers and equipment throughout a combat zone.

OCPA: Office of Coalition Provisional Authority. An agency created by the US Department of Defense for the purpose of rebuilding Iraq, and transitioning it to a democracy.

QRF: Quick Reaction Force. A unit of soldiers on call to respond to an attack on a military base in a deployed area.

R&R: Rest and Recuperation

RTO: Radio/Telephone Operator; usually monitors radio communication, but may also man a phone at a desk

SAM: Surface-to-Air Missile. Shoulder-fired rocket designed to shoot down aircraft.

TOC: Tactical Operations Center. The nerve center of a military unit where operations, intelligence and logistics are coordinated.